Finding God in the Body
A Spiritual Path for the Modern West

Benjamin A. Riggs

Finding God in the Body: A Spiritual Path for the Modern West
Copyright © 2016 Benjamin A. Riggs. All rights reserved.
Printed in the United States of America. No part of this
book may be used or reproduced in any manner
whatsoever without written permission from the author
except in cases of brief quotations.

www.FindingGodInTheBody.com

First edition of *Finding God in the Body: A Spiritual Path for the
Modern West* published in 2017.
Registered with Library of Congress United States
Copyright Office in 2015

ISBN: 0692760229
ISBN-13: 978-0692760222

Cover art and Albert Einstein graphic quote designed by
Michael Scott. Cover adapted from Da Vinci's *Vitruvian
Man*.

A human being is a part of a **WHOLE,** called by us the **UNIVERSE** —a part limited in **TIME** and **SPACE.** He experiences himself, his **THOUGHTS,** and **FEELINGS,** as something separated from the rest - a kind of optical **DELUSION** of his **CONSCIOUSNESS.** This delusion is a kind of **PRISON** for us, restricting us to our personal **DESIRES** and to affection for a few persons nearest us. **OUR TASK** must be to **FREE OURSELVES** from this prison by widening our circles of **COMPASSION** to embrace all living creatures and the whole of **NATURE** in its beauty.

— Albert **EINSTEIN**

Table of Contents

Acknowledgments

Introduction 1

1 The Truth of Suffering 15
2 The Examined Life 26
3 The Backdrop of Impermanence 44
4 The Birth of the False-Self 50
5 Project Becoming 61
6 Refuge 68
7 The Space Between Fundamentalism and Atheism 75
8 Is it Not Written in Your Book? 104
9 Faith Without Practice is Dead 138
10 Prayer and the Temple 148
11 How to Meditate With the Body 159
12 The Freedom to Love 173
13 The Mind of God 189

About the Author

ACKNOWLEDGMENTS

"No one who achieves success does so without acknowledging the help of others. The wise and confident acknowledge this help with gratitude." ~ Alfred North Whitehead

My friends gave me the computer used to write this book for Christmas in 2010. They pulled their money together and bought it for me with the added word of encouragement, "Write!" So I want to thank Carlston Floyd, Nate Marshall, Ryan Pommier, Carter Hamm, and Paige Parker, my wife, who spearheaded the operation. Without the computer or the encouragement this book would not be possible. I owe a special debt of gratitude to Paige Parker and Carlston Floyd, both of whom have made personal sacrifices so I could pursue my goals. I am eternally grateful.

I would also like to acknowledge the contributions of Michael Scott, Sarah Roussel, and Lyndon Marcotte who helped with the editing process and development of this book. A special thanks is owed to Michael Scott, who also designed the cover art.

I owe a special thanks to Bennie Riggs, Connie Caruso, and Nancy Nicholson—my parents and mother-in-law—for being supportive over the years; Blake Corder and Daniel Core for reading through and helping me hammer out the details of this book; and the countless friends that have endured intense conversations with me, so—unbeknownst to them—I could flesh out the ideas and language expressed therein.

Finally, I would be remiss if I did not pause to acknowledge those to whom I am intellectually and spiritually indebted. Their names are spread throughout the pages of this book but there are a few that deserve special mention. The teachings of Thomas Merton, Chogyam Trungpa, and Reginald Ray have influenced me to such a degree that without them this book would not be possible. Merton opened my eyes to the depths of Western spirituality and Chogyam Trungpa acquainted me with the majesty of the human condition. But it was Dr. Ray that introduced me to the somatic spirituality that serves as the foundation of this book. In a world where spiritually is often reduced to mere belief and intellectual speculation, his emphasis on body-based practice stands apart as a unique contribution. Furthermore, Dr. Ray took the time to personally cultivate this awareness within me. So, I owe a special thanks to him and hope that my gratitude is reflected in every word that follows.

INTRODUCTION

"Do not seek to follow in the footsteps of the wise. Seek what they sought." ~ Basho

This book is an attempt to flesh out a functional spirituality for the modern West. By this I mean a transformative system of practice supplemented by an inner-mythos that speaks to the sensibilities of modern man. This is not an academic endeavor for me—it is my path, for I am a modern Western man and as such, my worldview is heavily influenced by the often divergent forces of Christianity, Eastern philosophy, and modern science.

I was born in Louisiana. In the Bible Belt, religion and science share a contentious border. The brand of Christianity I saw growing up did not interest me. So I looked to the wisdom and practices of the East, which in the age of the internet is closer than the church around the corner. I became interested in Tibetan Buddhism but there was something missing. In Tibetan Buddhism there is a heavy emphasis on meditation practice and a rich philosophical tradition, both of which were deeply rewarding. But the belief in reincarnation and the pantheon of exotic deities did not resonate with me. My heart just wasn't in it. I never parted ways with Buddhist practice, but my path did eventually bring me back to the teachings of Christianity. I say my path brought me back, but in truth it introduced me to Christianity for the first time. My Buddhist background enabled me to cut through the fundamentalist veneer to the contemplative core of Christianity where I found an inner-mythos that resonated with me.

When I was four or five my family moved to a small town in East Texas. I was a typical kid: I loved airplanes, dinosaurs, and spaceships. I was also quite fond of church. On Sunday mornings these interests overlapped as I sat in the pews of the local Baptist Church drawing dinosaurs, rockets, and airplanes on the back of offering envelopes.

My family was not religious, so I often went to church alone. This wasn't a problem for me because I got to ride the church bus. The highlight of my week was sitting on the bus next to a young man with Down Syndrome who liked to sing the Bob Seger song, "Old Time Rock-and-Roll." In my early years, I loved church and everything about it.

My love for church proved to be conditional. When I was in the first grade my parents divorced, and my church-going days came to a screeching halt. I blamed God for the failure of my family. I expected him to look after me and my interests in exchange for devotion and church attendance. Every Sunday I heard that God watches over his flock, that he takes care of his own. Since I believed and my butt was in the pew, I counted myself as a member of the flock. When my parents separated, I felt overlooked, which either meant God was a liar or he did not exist. Either way, I had no use for him.

Following the divorce, I was no longer the fun loving, good-hearted kid who liked to draw dinosaurs and spaceships. I became angry and did not know how to express my anger. My family split up and there was nothing I could do about it. My sister went to live with my mother and I moved back to Louisiana with my dad.

One night while my father and I were watching *America's Funniest Home Videos*, he caught staring out the window at a group of kids playing football. He insisted I go out and make some new friends. I didn't want to, but he made me. So I walked down the stairs from our apartment building to the courtyard where they were playing. I picked the biggest kid in the bunch, walked up to him, and spit in his face. Then, I realized what I had done and took off running! He tracked me down and beat me within an inch of my life.

The next ten to twelve years of my life were dark. At an early age, I learned I was alone. No one was looking out for me. There was no God and no family, nothing to fall back on. I had to look after myself. That's not to say I wasn't well cared for. I had everything I needed and got more than most, but I still struggled. I did not know how to cope with life. This mounting frustration made my first encounters with alcohol welcomed occasions.

Alcohol medicated my fear and anger. Drinking was how I coped—and I coped a lot. Alcohol wasn't my problem; it was my solution. It was the antidote to fear, the countermeasure for anger, and the lubricant that enabled me to overcome my social anxiety. And it seemed to work. I felt like I was back on course, but this course turned out to be a slippery slope.

At the ripe old age of seventeen, my dad sent me to

Canton, Texas for substance abuse treatment. When the counselors confronted me about my drinking and drug use I said, "This is how all teenage boys from Louisiana act. The only problem I have is that my parents won't get off my back." I was not the least bit interested in what treatment had to offer because I didn't think I had a problem.

Technically, I still wasn't sober. Not long after my parent's divorce a psychiatrist diagnosed me with ADD/ADHD. Adderall is an addictive stimulant used to treat behavioral problems in hyperactive children. I was a hyper active kid with a sleuth of behavioral problems, so they prescribed me Adderall. I took it most of my childhood, excluding a stint that followed a run in with the law. When I was twelve years old, I got caught selling my Adderall at school. The prescription was revoked for a time but eventually refilled, and I was taking it when I arrived in Canton—although, I was not taking it as prescribed. The treatment staff caught me hiding it in my cheek and bringing it back to my room where I would snort it. As a result, the staff doctor took me off of Adderall. For the first time since I was twelve, I could not get my hands on either drugs or alcohol. I couldn't check out. I couldn't cope.

Treatment forced me to relate to life with no anesthetic. It felt like I was losing my mind. Out of desperation I stole some coffee packets from the cafeteria. In a room search the staff found the packets in my desk drawer. They questioned my roommates and learned that I was snorting coffee in the bathroom. When they took me off of Adderall, I started to reach. I did not know how to live sober. I was willing to do anything to flee the rawness and immediacy of life. When they confronted me about the coffee, my game was up. I could no longer deny I had a problem. I couldn't continue to say, "This is how all teenage boys from Louisiana act," because I did not know another teenage boy from Louisiana—or anywhere else, for that matter—snorting coffee. Now that I was bent over a barrel, they began talking to me about God.

When it came to God, I did not parse my words. I thought God was something stupid people used to explain their problems away. I made it clear that I had no use for God. Sure, I caused plenty of problems for myself, but God was just as useless in my eyes. The treatment center staff arranged for me to meet a man named Billy Jack. I was pretty apprehensive, but equally excited. I despised the idea of God. My hatred for God made debating his existence enjoyable. I wanted the person I was debating to feel the same hatred and disappointment I felt. I thought I could transfer my pain to the other person by defeating them in debate. However, Billy Jack took another angle with me, perhaps the only angle that would have worked at the time.

Billy Jack did not try to prove anything to me. He spoke to me about possibilities, not certainties. We never talked philosophy, dogma, or theology. In fact, we hardly talked. The conversation only lasted about six or seven minutes. It began with me going on your typical resentment-filled rant against God and religion. That lasted about five minutes. Then, conquered by boredom, he interrupted to ask me two simple questions.

First Billy Jack asked, "Is it possible that God exists?" He did not push his beliefs onto me. He simply asked if God was a possibility in my mind. To this point, I conceded. I could not disprove the existence of God any more than he could prove it.

So, I said, "It is highly unlikely, but possible." Then Billy Jack asked, "At this point in your life is there anything more important than exploring that possibility?" Again, I had to concede, but not for the reasons you might imagine.

This was my second stint in treatment. Spirituality is a central component of most recovery programs and both of the centers I visited emphasized God. My patience with God was wearing thin. I wanted to try something else, but in treatment you are branded "closed-minded" if you reject something without first trying it. I figured that if I tried it and it didn't work, they might offer me something else. So I said, "I will say your prayers and read your books, because when nothing changes—and nothing is going to change—this will prove that God is a joke." He replied, "That's good enough for me," and walked away. I never saw him again.

At the time, I had no idea how impactful that conversation would be on me. The course of my life was forever changed by that brief exchange. If I start with who I am right now and trace it back, the encounter with Billy Jack would be the greatest aberration along my life's trajectory. He did not convert me or even convince me that God is real. I was not impressed by his argument. He opened my mind. Billy Jack got me to step out of what I thought and see the world from another point of view. He introduced another vantage point.

Initially, my intense disdain for all things Christian did not enable me to approach a church, the Bible, or even the concept of God. My search began in the East. I had to figure out how to live sober and manage my hyperactivity without Adderall. One of the staff members thought meditation might be helpful and gave me a book about Buddhism. I understood little of what I read but the little I understood, I held onto for dear life. Before long, I was a card-carrying Buddhist.

At first, Buddhism was just a costume. The Dalai Lama was the only Buddhist I had ever seen—I'd read a couple of his books and saw him on television a time or two. As far as I was concerned, he was the official face of Buddhism. So, I did everything in my power to look and act like him.

Upon leaving treatment, I moved to a sober-living home in South Florida. There I was in Boca Raton—a seventeen year old, 6' 8" Buddhist redneck from Shreveport, Louisiana. I was walking down the street with a freshly shaved head and flip flops trying my best to be Buddhist as hell—dramatically stepping over ants, eating veggie lo-mein, and counting the beads on my mala while mindlessly reciting the mantra *Om Mani Padme Hung* and chewing tobacco. I always believed that happiness was something I had to cook up, and at this point in my life that belief had not changed. I just had a new cookbook.

I started to read everything I could get my hands on about Buddhism. I observed certain codes of conduct—I abstained from alcohol and drugs, didn't eat meat, and practiced meditation. During my stay in Boca Raton I learned how to meditate from the Roshi at a local Zen temple. Meditation enabled my mind to settle, but I still didn't see the link between spirituality and my daily life. I intellectually understood the connection, but I did not practice it. Spirituality was a private affair. I read my books and practiced meditation and *then* I went about my day. I wouldn't make the connection between practice and daily life for several more years.

Fast forward five years: I'm back home in Louisiana, and my girlfriend and I are at a Mardi Gras parade. I've been practicing meditation for a while and have read a number of books about spirituality. As a result, I thought the mysteries of the universe had exposed themselves to me. This inflated self-image came crumbling down when my girlfriend uttered two simple words: "He's cute." Those two words triggered an explosive reaction within me. In front of God and everyone, I turned and spat in her face.

Relationships were difficult for me. I was terrified of rejection and extremely clingy. I always thought my partner was looking for a way out. When she said, "He's cute," I turned to see who she was talking about. "He looks an awful lot like her ex-boyfriend," I thought. Long ago I identified him as the man she would leave me for. This incident sparked fear within me, which quickly turned to rage. Then, I spat. For a moment, I was stripped naked. It embarrassed the hell out of me. She stared at me in disbelief before walking away.

Spitting in her face proved to be one of the greatest revelations of my short life. In that moment, it became unequivocally clear to me and the people around me that I was full of crap. All the books I read, my vegetarian diet, and Buddhist tattoos—none of it mattered. When confronted by fear, anger, and jealousy my spirituality fell like a house of cards. The self-image I bought into and sold to others was a façade. I was the same angry child who stormed out of church and spat in the face of that kid in the courtyard. I still had no idea how to cope with life.

This insight was not some glorious moment that placed me on a pink cloud of bliss. It was devastating. I was humiliated and did not know what to do. I knew drinking and drugs were of no help. Once again, I was suspicious of all things "spiritual" but did not know where else to look. So I cracked open one of my books about Tibetan Buddhism. There I read about the practice of *Tonglen*. This wasn't the first I heard of *Tonglen*, but it was the first time I ever practiced it. Before I thought I was too advanced for *Tonglen*. I thought I was beyond fear and resentment. Now, I knew better.

In the practice of Tonglen you visualize someone you are resentful at and imagine yourself breathing in their suffering, symbolized by a black smoke. With the exhalation you breathe out a white smoke that represents the causes of happiness, which they inhale. So I did this practice with the two people I resented most, my girlfriend and her ex-boyfriend. And the resentment began to subside. After a few weeks of daily Tonglen practice the fear and anger fell away. This was the first time my spirituality and daily life came together.

I knew what I was looking for was within me and that daily practice was the only way to find it, but subconsciously I believed there was a shortcut. Daily practice is hard work and takes a long time. I wanted something more magical. I wanted to leave the rigors of practice and daily life behind and escape to a spiritual Shangri-La where enlightenment is obtained through osmosis. This sounded like a monastery to me. The strict structure, intense practice, and long hours of study did not figure into my idea of monastic life. I imagined a monastery as a kind of Buddha factory—you went in one side all messed up and came out the other side enlightened! The only problem my monastic escape plan presented was location. All the Buddhist enlightenment factories seemed to be in Asia.

About this time, I was introduced to the great Catholic mystic Thomas Merton. Through his writings I discovered a side of Christianity not often seen in the Bible Belt. He introduced me to the contemplative dimension of Christianity, which has depth and is more concerned with daily life than the hereafter. At times his Christian language rubbed me the wrong way, but his powerful writing style, profound insight, and masterful use of symbolism resonated with me on a deeper level than did Buddhist lingo. So, I began studying contemplative Christianity.

I befriended a local priest who was familiar with Merton and was himself a Franciscan friar. He helped me to better understand the contemplative side of Christianity, and how to apply spiritual principles to my life. When I told him about my plans to enter a monastery, he suggested a trial run. He made arrangements for me to stay at a Franciscan Friary in Ava, Missouri, which shared a property with a Trappist monastery, the order to which Merton belonged. This gave me the chance to test the waters of monastic life without having to commit to Asia just yet.

I cannot stress enough the value of my trip to Assumption Abbey. There I met the most whole and complete men I had ever known. For me, spirituality was a superficial endeavor. It had more to do with changing my self-image than true transformation. But these men were transformed. They were living it. Standing before me was a group of men who embodied exactly what I was looking for. So naturally, I hopped on a plane and flew clear across the world in search of what I just found!

Any illusions of a Shangri-La were promptly shattered upon arriving in India. The overwhelming frustration I experienced after being involved in what amounted to a kidnapping and credit card fraud, plus the sheer culture shock, popped my fantastical bubble. Don't get me wrong, India is an amazing place—I would go back in a heartbeat—but it was not what I expected. Obviously, this was not India's fault. I was looking to escape, and I brought with me the one thing I wanted to leave behind: myself.

Fortunately, I picked a less populated part of India and went during the offseason. I had no one to talk to, no TV to watch. I was without distraction for the first time in my life. It was a beautiful accident. I was forced upon myself. Most of my time was spent reading and meditating. I would also go to the monastery and listen to lectures about Buddhist philosophy and meditation. And I was fortunate enough to meet someone who had devoted their life to contemplative spirituality and was willing to work with me.

One morning I was walking down the winding mountain road that connected Dharamkot and McLeod Ganj. I regularly went up into the mountain caves and spent a couple of days in retreat. One day, on the way down the mountain, I saw a monk standing on the side of the road. In broken English he asked, "Do you want learn meditate?" That was my first meeting with Jetsun Thubpten.

Jetsun was a Buddhist hermit who had spent the last twelve years living in the mountains. After two decades in one of the largest Tibetan monastic colleges, he concluded that study was insufficient. He wanted to live a life of practice. So he left Sera

Mey monastery and took to a life of solitude and meditation.

Jetsun and I sat together for two hours every other day. We would meditate, eat, and talk. Jetsun taught me that meditation was not limited to the cushion, but was alive in everything we do. He used to say, "If you can't meditate while you cook, eat, and shit, you can't meditate!" Mostly Jetsun taught by way of example—not fancy lectures or philosophical discourse. In Jetsun, spirituality and daily life were one and the same.

The physical and spiritual are not opposed to each other. They are not two competing worlds. There is not something apart from our life called the "spiritual journey." The journey is our life. When we sleepwalk through life, we are just along for the ride. When we mindfully participate in the journey, we are walking the spiritual path. Like the men at Assumption Abbey, Jetsun was awake.

I wanted to stay in India. Jetsun asked, "For what?" I hemmed and hawed around for a minute before replying, "To learn more about meditation and Buddhist spirituality and maybe," I awkwardly added, "teach Western tourists passing through India about meditation." Jetsun smiled through my confusion and jokingly said, "We don't need any more Gurus!" Then he told me, "If you want to teach Westerners meditation, you should go back to the West where Westerners live." So here I am, eleven years later, sharing my experience as a Westerner walking the spiritual path.

Jiddu Krishnamurti once said, "We are all the story of humanity." This story is written in our body. We must sit down and read the pages of our heart. In this book, I share not only what I have learned from studying myself, but—and more importantly—the path of practice that has enabled me to study myself.

Spirituality is at a crossroads in the West. We are looking for a practical path that resonates with our modern, Western mind. This is difficult to find because it is not readily available. Therefore, the main objective of this book is to introduce the reader to a path structure. Such a structure must speak directly to our suffering and its causes, as well as the transcendent potential embedded in the human condition (Chapters 1-6). It must also incorporate an inner-mythos that appeals to our heart without offending the modern sensibilities of the Western mind (Chapters 7-8). And no path structure would be complete without a system of practice that enables the individual to move beyond the false-self and reconnect with the richness of their True Life as it is revealed in the body (Chapters 9-13).

The great Zen master D.T. Suzuki wrote, "So long as the masters are indulging in negations, denials, contradictions, or paradoxes, the stain of speculation is not quite washed off them."[1] I do not pretend to be a master, nor do I believe this book is free of such indulgences. However, I hope that with every word I write, someone finds the inspiration to dig deeper. There is an inner voice calling us out of the claustrophobic world of the false-self, inviting us to reunite with the life of the body. This book outlines the path of practice and the inner-mythos that has enabled me to answer that call and I hope it empowers the reader to do the same. It is to this end that I dedicate *Finding God in the Body: A Spiritual Path for the Modern West*.

---

[1] Shunryu Suzuki, *Selected Writings of D.T. Suzuki*, "Practical Methods of Zen Instruction," Doubleday (1956), pg 122

1 THE TRUTH OF SUFFERING

> *"You cannot really eliminate pain through aggression. The more you kill, the more you strengthen the killer who will create new things to be killed. The aggression grows until finally there is no space: the whole environment has been solidified. There are not even gaps at which to look back or to do a double take. The whole space has become completely filled with aggression."* ~*Chogyam Trungpa* [1]

No one intentionally creates problems for themselves. We all want to be happy. "That everyone desires happiness for himself or herself is an incontestable fact," writes Mortimer J. Adler, the prolific American philosopher. "In everyone's vocabulary the word 'happiness' stands for something always sought for its own sake and never as a means to anything beyond itself. No one can complete the sentence 'I want happiness because I want...'"[2] Happiness is the aim of every life.

---

[1] Chogyam Trungpa, The Myth of Freedom and the Way of Meditation, Shambhala (2001), pg. 51
[2] Mortimer J. Adler, *We Hold These Truths*, Macmillan Publishing Company (1987), pg. 52

In this sense, happiness refers not to the satisfaction of fleeting desires, but to a full and complete life—contentment. This deeper happiness is elusive. For many of us it remains out of reach. Life feels like a never-ending project. We are forever trying to improve our self, our job, our relationships, and no matter how hard we try, happiness escapes us. This is because our search for happiness focuses on the outside world. It takes us out of our Self.

Spirituality is a path of action that reconnects us with the vitality of the body. In this sense, spiritual practice is transformative. Spiritual practice moves beyond belief and theory and into the realm of action where change takes place. The desire to change comes from suffering. No one wants to change unless they are dissatisfied. They might read a few self-help books, but they will not commit themselves to the difficult work of transformation unless they are motivated by suffering.

The word *suffering* sounds heavy-handed, but here it has a subtler connotation. In its most basic form, suffering is the subliminal belief that we are missing something. We feel empty, broken, incomplete, or just plain bored with the life we are living and yearn for something more. So we go to church, a yoga class, or learn to meditate hoping to find a more meaningful life. Our exploration of spirituality starts with suffering because suffering brings us to spirituality. The Buddha said as much when he began his presentation of the spiritual path with the Truth of Suffering.[3]

---

[3] The Four Noble Truths are the essence of the Buddha's teachings. They are the truth of suffering, the truth of the cause of suffering, the truth of the end of suffering, and the truth of the path that leads to the end of suffering.

The Buddha wasn't looking at life like the glass was half empty when he taught the Truth of Suffering. He was stating the obvious: suffering is a universal experience, common to all people. Spirituality is deeply concerned with the reality of our day-to-day lives, and suffering is a part of our life. Therefore, an authentic spirituality turns into suffering, rather than away from it. The first step on the spiritual path is an examination of suffering.

The truth of suffering suggests that happiness evades us because it is found in the one place we have been unwilling to look. We have looked everywhere, except for within ourselves. To change the way we relate to the world, we must address the point at which we depart from it. Suffering is that point of departure. We turn away from our life at the first sign of discomfort. For that reason, suffering is an enigma to many of us. We have little insight into the movement of suffering. We are familiar with the superficial narrative that accompanies our pain and disappointment, but are baffled as to why we fall back into those self-defeating patterns time and again.

The Suffering of Our Suffering

Suffering is a process, not an event. It moves through three distinct stages: the suffering of our suffering, the suffering of change, and pervasive suffering. We will start our inquiry with what we know best, the suffering of our suffering. While we might be ignorant to suffering's deeper dimensions, we are all too aware of the heartache, fear, and anger that erupt on the surface. We know that explosive blend of frustration and sadness that comes welling up when we find ourselves back where we started, yet again: should we scream or curse, run away, break something, or just sit down and have a good cry? We feel defeated. This is the "suffering of our suffering"—the blunt pain that characterizes everything from tragedy to a bad day. But it does not stop there.

Suffering is cyclic. We suffer *over* our suffering, or play the victim role. We get caught up in self-pity and lament our misfortunes, crying out, "Why me?" "Why?" you ask? Because wanting something to be other than it is does not make it so.

In the midst of pain, we often make personal resolutions. We frantically swear off the supposed sources of our discontentment, saying, "I'm deleting his number; I will not drink anymore; I'll never eat like that again." All of our resolutions have one basic message, "I am done!" While this revulsion may be natural and sane, our reaction is childish and naïve. It is an immature mind that believes years of self-defeating patterns are overcome by throwing our arms up and exclaiming, "I'm done!"

Wanting to stop does not lead to transformation. What is an addiction apart from the perpetuation of an unwanted behavior? The idea that swearing off overcomes suffering is an adult version of the adolescent attitude that, following our first break-up declares, "Love stinks! I will never date again." We are trying to protect ourselves from pain instead of listening to it. "I am done," means, "I am out of here!" This is the point of departure. It is where we turn away from life.

The Suffering of Change

There is more to suffering than the pain and drama floating around on the surface. But since that is where we typically tuck tail and run, we are oblivious to the subterranean forces of suffering. When we sit with our pain instead of running, it becomes obvious that there is more than meets the eye. There is an underlying pattern. Suffering is a cycle of unwanted behavior. We relapse into these self-defeating patterns because beneath the surface there is a current pulling us in that direction. That undertow is our conditioning.

We have trained ourselves to check out. "Every single habitual pattern has been developed in relationship to an experience that was intolerable for us," says Dr. Reginald Ray, one of the great Buddhist teachers of the West. These habitual patterns take us out of ourselves in search of relief, which gives rise to the suffering of change.

The suffering of change is triggered by the belief that happiness is found outside of ourselves—that some person, object, or bit of knowledge is the missing ingredient. These cycles are perpetuated by ignorance—as in, we are *ignoring* the facts. We are so excited by our latest fling that *we fail to remember* our last five flings were also billed as "the one." We ignore our experience and cue up the mental obsession, convincing ourselves, yet again, that our lives *could* be improved by a new job or a new relationship. Separated from the truth of our experience, we attach ourselves to the new career, life strategy, or boyfriend in the hope that this will be "the one."

In the beginning, this wishful thinking seems to be confirmed: we get hopped up about our new self-improvement strategy; we stay awake half the night talking on the phone with our newfound soul mate; we put on our best outfit and show up to the new job with a little hitch in our giddy-up. All of this excitement creates a diversion. It masks the underlying sense of dissatisfaction. But then comes the sudden change: it isn't new anymore! We desensitize to the object of our attachment and it loses the power to distract us from the truth of our suffering. The stress starts to build as we realize the job expects more of us than we can give. The latest life strategy is revealed to be the same ol' stuff repackaged with new language. The partner who, two months ago, was the answer to all our prayers becomes the reason we are praying! We expected them to be our answer—to always make us feel wanted, needed, and valuable. Now we silence their calls.

These cycles are precipitated by a common misunderstanding. We believe that external factors create our suffering. The belief that others cause our pain implies they also cause our happiness. So we get sucked into the business of trying to arrange the world to suit ourselves. Much to our dismay, our solutions become the frustration, heartache, and disappointment they were intended to remedy. As the 8th century Buddhist master Shantideva said, "We hate suffering, but love its causes."[4]

We look for the cure in the causes of our ailments. We thought he or she was our "other half." We expected that relationship to "complete" us. This seemed like a good idea when, during the honeymoon phase of the relationship, we were filled with warm bubbly feelings. But those feelings are not a solution; they are a distraction. They divert our attention away from the deep-seated, seemingly incurable void in our heart.

---

[4] Shantideva, *The Bodhisattva's Guide to the Way of Life* Shambala (2006), pg. 83

Pervasive Suffering

The search for a solution is triggered by the idea that deep-down there is a problem. This is suffering in its most basic form: pervasive suffering. It's the subliminal belief that we aren't enough: not good enough, smart enough, or loveable enough. Pervasive suffering is a form of shame. It tells us we are missing something that everyone else has; something we are *supposed* to have. So what are we missing? Perhaps a story from the Zen tradition can shed light on this question.

Long ago, a famous Zen master passed away. Thousands gathered at his monastery to mourn the loss. His chief disciple and successor sat on the steps of the temple crying. One of his peers approached him and said, "You have to stop crying. You are the heir to our master. If people see you sobbing, they will think you are not enlightened and unfit to lead." The student replied, "Let them think what they will. When I am sad, I cry. If that means I am not enlightened, then I am not enlightened."

Even the Buddha cries. Sadness is an unavoidable part of life. When we try to avoid the unavoidable, we tear away from reality, which is revealed in the basic awareness of the body. When we turn away from our sadness, we turn away from the life of the body. Our True Life is rejected in favor of a new life. This second life is the imaginary world between our ears. We become identified with thought and the unity of mind and body is ruptured. The migration from the heart to the head leaves us feeling incomplete or discontented—without content or meaning. When we separate ourselves from the life of the body, we feel dead inside. Therefore, disembodiment is the basis of pervasive suffering.

The feeling that we are broken or missing something fuels the cycle of suffering. It transforms our life into a scavenger hunt—a frantic search for that magical missing ingredient (the suffering of change), which always ends in disappointment (the suffering of our suffering). Pervasive suffering takes us out of our Self in search of happiness. We feel undone or incomplete and turn to money, relationships, or entertainment, instead of within. As a result, we squander away our lives pounding on a door, demanding to be let into a house we never left.

Listening to Suffering

The spiritual path takes a different approach to suffering. We have spent a great deal of time looking for happiness, but we have not found what we are looking for despite our best efforts. The truth of suffering asks, "Have we been unable to find what we are looking for because we were looking in the wrong place? Is happiness found in the one place we've been unwilling to look?" The one place we have refused to look is within ourselves. Therefore, it stands to reason that what we are looking for is hidden within the walls of our body.

Spirituality isn't wishful thinking. Rattling off clichés will not do the trick. Belief and intellectual knowledge alone will not suffice. We have to go further. Transformation requires action. It takes practice. We have to learn *how to* sit with our experience: the good, the bad, and the boring. This skill is called meditation.

The Practice of Meditation

In basic meditation practice, we are moving beyond what we think and reconnecting with the body of direct experience. We are not trying to figure suffering out or fix it; nor are we trying to silence our mind. We watch the mind as it turns the present moment into a problem and entertains itself by chasing after a solution to the problem it just created. But rather than seeing this as a problem to be solved, just notice it and return to the present moment.

In meditation, we see that suffering is a game, of sorts. We do not need to destroy the game. We need to observe it. It is important that we see the game for what it is. It is fine that our thinking mind plays the game. We get into trouble when we take the game too seriously. Trying to destroy the game is just another example of taking it too seriously. So, meditation practice works with our seriousness, not the game per se. Meditation looks within, which is the practice of insight. Insight exposes the gap between reality and our thoughts. As a result, the seriousness we attribute to our thoughts diminishes.

Many people say that meditation isn't for them. They *think*, "My mind is all over the place. I can't sit still. I *think* too much to meditate." But that is the game talking. The thinking mind can turn something as simple as sitting on the floor into a problem. This isn't proof that meditation is a bad fit. This is the very thing meditation is intended to address. It means that meditation is the perfect fit for you!

Meditation works with the problem-solving mind by sitting through the belief that there is a problem. We sit with the speed and aggression of what the Buddhist tradition calls the "monkey-mind." This doesn't always feel good. Spiritual practice is a discipline, and sometimes discipline asks us to do what is difficult. This cultivates our ability to delay gratification and sit with our discomfort.

In meditation, we commit to reality by renouncing our escape plans. We will not stop running away from our suffering until we see there is nowhere to run. There are no other options, just *what is*. To retreat into *what is not* is to slip into self-deception, which is the way of suffering.

Meditation is a practice of loneliness. When we sit, we sit with ourselves. In silence we are all alone. There is no backdrop upon which to project blame and no board to pin our expectations upon. There is *no one* to blame and nothing to save us. Blame and expectation bind us to suffering. They paralyze us, leaving us sitting in self-pity while we wait for the world to change, so we can be happy. When we see we are all alone, we realize that we are responsible for our lives. At this point, the belief that we are stuck falls away and we start growing.

***

To begin the practice, take a seat on a cushion or in a chair. Settle into a comfortable posture with your chest open and back straight. Place your hands in your lap or palms down on your thighs. Allow your head to be at ease.

Bring your awareness to the sensation of the breath at the tip of the nose. When the mind drifts off into thought, label it "thinking." Do not beat yourself up for thinking too much. Simply return to the breath at the tip of the nose.

After a while, you may experience a sense of panic, like you can't sit there for another second. This is the suffering of our suffering. Just reconnect with the breath and continue to sit. Soon, a stream of burning thoughts will assault you, each expressing an urgent need to get up and do something: mow the grass, do the laundry, finish a project. This is the suffering of change. Return to the breath. Finally, you will be overwhelmed by a profound sense of discomfort, a seeming inability to sit with yourself. You will feel uncomfortable in your own skin. This is pervasive suffering. Continue to sit, not ignoring, but simply noticing whatever arises. It might be uncomfortable, possibly even agonizing, but do not fixate on the discomfort or try to repair it. Just sit.

How do you just sit? Return to the simplicity of the breath. Feel yourself relaxing down into the body. Do not let the world be reduced to the tunnel vision of the thinking mind. Notice the chirping birds, the passing cars, and the itching sensation on the tip of your nose— all of which arises within the awareness of the body. Do not analyze the birds, cars, or itch; just notice. Allow your awareness to pour out into the fullness of who you are. Simply honor whatever arises with basic awareness and return to the breath—"touch and go," as Chogyam Trungpa used to say.

For our practice to be effective it must be consistent. The length of each session is not as important as the frequency. If we sit twice a day for 15 minutes, the length will expand over time. Eventually, 15 minutes will become 20, 25, and then 30 minutes. Accountability is important part of consistency, which is why many people find meditation groups helpful. Group accountability calls us back to the cushion. If you cannot find a meditation group in your area, search your acquaintances for people interested in starting one. You can use the instructions above as guidelines. Now we will look deeper into our suffering with the practice of self-analysis.

2 THE EXAMINED LIFE

"Examine yourself from every side. Note harmful thoughts and every futile striving. Thus it is that the awakened beings on the spiritual path apply the remedies to keep a steady mind." ~ Shantideva [1]

In the book quoted above, Shantideva asks, "Is it easier to cover the world with leather or to put on a pair of shoes?" Most of us are quick to proclaim the latter, but in practice subscribe to the former. "Everyone thinks of changing the world," said Tolstoy, "but no one thinks of changing himself." We give lip service to the idea that we cannot change others, but spend most of our time trying to arrange the world to suit ourselves. This leaves us frustrated because we are the only person we can change. As the old saying goes, "It is better to find one fault in yourself than 1,000 faults in someone else."

Frustration is a sign of powerlessness—the belief that we are stuck. Though common, the belief that we're stuck is an illusion. We are never stuck. "Stuck" is a symptom of the victim mentality that blames the world for our problems. Blame sits around waiting on others to change so we can be happy. It covers the earth with leather. When we take this approach, we

---

[1] Shantideva, *The Bodhisattva's Guide to the Way of Life* (Shambala 2006), pg. 69

cover everything except for ourselves, which leaves us feeling stagnant. It chains us to our misery.

In reality, we are not stuck. Happiness and suffering—peace, fear, love, anger, joy, jealousy, clarity, stress, depression, freedom, and addiction—arise from internal causes and conditions.[2] When we bring our awareness back to ourselves—when we drive all blame into ourselves—we begin moving. We put on shoes.

Everybody wants to be happy and free of suffering. It is not a question of motivation, but of direction. If we look outside ourselves for the causes of our suffering, frustration follows. If we look at ourselves, we make progress. The proper function of the intellect is not to judge others, but to search ourselves for beliefs and behaviors that deviate from the truth of who we are. So when we apply the intellect to this end, we grow.

The Maintenance of Conscience

When we take our judgmental mind—the mind that is so good at finding fault in others—and turn it in on itself, we start to walk the path. This can be tricky because the mind trends toward self-deception when left to its own devices. It is difficult to find fault in our self when the mind in question is conducting the analysis. We need an approach that ties the mind to truth.

The practice of self-analysis tethers the mind to reality. For this reason, the anonymous author of the *Cloud of Unknowing* begins chapter twenty-eight of his classical text on contemplative prayer by stating that "a man should not proceed in this work

---

[2] Isaiah 45:7

before he has cleansed his conscience."[3] The maintenance of conscience is an integral part of the spiritual journey, though it is often neglected.

It may be tempting to overlook the practice of self-analysis. Please think twice before you do so. Many seekers disregard their psychological well-being. They pretend that highfalutin' states of mind are the name of the game. When we ignore our psychological condition, we are looking for a shortcut. There are no shortcuts on the spiritual path. Shortcuts are traps. They attempt to bypass the uncomfortable stages of the journey. In the end, the repressed material resurfaces and ambushes us. The shadow knows where the cracks are, and like water, it follows the path of least resistance. So, contemplative spirituality begins with identifying those patterns of consciousness and behavior that cast us from our center out to the perimeter where we live as a false-self.

Many of us live on the perimeter, alienated from the depths of our inner-life. As a result, we are identified with an exterior image. This exterior image is the false-self. It is the image we project to the world. Spirituality is a return to our center. It is a process of letting go of the false-self and its exterior strategies for happiness. But we cannot give up what we do not possess. We come to possess the false-self through awareness.

"You are always a slave to what you're not aware of," writes the Jesuit teacher Fr. Anthony de Mello. "When you are aware of it, you're free from it."[4] Currently, we are unaware of the false-self. We think about it incessantly, but do not see it with the unbiased eye of basic awareness. Since we identify with the

---

[3] Anonymous author, *Cloud of Unknowing*, Doubleday (1996), pg. 75
[4] Fr. Anthony de Mello, *Awareness*, Doubleday (1996), pg. 71

false-self, we are too close to see it clearly. We do not *know* that it is false—that it is a mask. As a result, we are a slave to its every demand. We take it too seriously. When we see it as false, we stop responding to its commands. In this way, awareness facilitates transformation. But where do we begin? At the risk of stating the obvious, I must answer that we start where we are.

Humility and the Practice of Self Analysis

Before undertaking a journey, we have to locate ourselves on the map. The practice of self-analysis pinpoints our location. It cultivates humility. Humility is an honest understanding of *who* we are and *where* we are at. This is the absolute starting point for all spiritual practice. We are deceiving ourselves, if we try to start anywhere other than where we are. There are no advanced beginners.

Humility is a fidelity to truth. "Truth is something so noble," says the great Catholic mystic Meister Eckhart, "that if God could turn aside from it, I would keep Truth and let God go." When it comes to truth, there can be no compromise. As the old Jewish proverb goes, "A half truth is a whole lie." When our life is a half truth, it is a whole lie.

Perfect honesty is a tall order. But if progress is our goal, "we shall need to raise our eyes toward perfection, and be ready to walk in that direction," writes Bill Wilson, the founder of Alcoholics Anonymous.[5] In this sense, perfection has nothing to do with our ideas, expectations, or ambitions. That is perfectionism. Spiritual perfection is not defined by external demands. It is the heartfelt desire to be true to our Self and the

---

[5] Bill Wilson, *Twelve Steps and Twelve Traditions,* Alcoholics Anonymous World Services (2012), p. 68

degree of willingness with which we respond to that desire. The willingness to be honest with ourselves is the practical foundation of humility.

Honesty isn't just an objective. There is process involved. We need to learn *how to* be honest—how to accept what comes up for us, both the good and the bad. Self-analysis is a method that enables us to get honest with ourselves about where we stand in relationship to our values. There is a gulf that separates who we are and the life we are *actually* living. The practice of self-analysis exposes that gulf.

"When we point a searching finger down our throats to analyze the nature of our previous ways," writes Khedrup Je, the first Panchen Lama,[6] "we see a fox wearing a lion's skin. We yearn for Truth, but don't really practice it." This inner-fox, so to speak, is the false-self we project. When we lay our life out in black-and-white, we hold up a mirror. Only what is real is reflected in the mirror. When we look at our life in black-and-white, we do not see the reflection of our false-self. In this way, the practice of self-analysis tethers the mind to reality.

Self-analysis can take several forms. I will go over two methods. Both are practical and effective, though each meets us with a different level of intensity. We will begin with the most exhaustive form of self-analysis which includes a personal inventory, admission, internal restitution, and amends. Then we will proceed to the practice of journaling.

Personal Inventory

Every contemplative tradition, from Catholicism to

---

[6] The Panchen Lama is the second highest ranking lama in the Gelug school of Tibetan Buddhism (behind the Dalai Lama).

Buddhism, recognizes the need to start with confession or purification. These practices are the gateway to the contemplative life. One should not enter the temple without first clearing their conscience.[7] The journey always begins with an in-depth personal inventory followed at once by a conversation with our spiritual friend—a mentor, teacher, priest, or an understanding companion.

The practice offered below is found in the Twelve Steps of Alcoholics Anonymous.[8] Though the spirituality of Alcoholics Anonymous was originally intended for those struggling with alcoholism, its Twelve Steps have made an indelible impact on Western spirituality. The well-known Franciscan priest, Fr. Richard Rohr said, "The spirituality of Alcoholics Anonymous, as it was first called, is going to go down as the significant and authentic American contribution to the history of spirituality."[9] Though the Twelve Steps were conceived with alcoholics in mind, their unique blend of pragmatism and depth make them useful to us all. This is particularly true of Steps Four through Nine which provide us with a simple and effective way to remove the debris of our unexamined life.

To begin our personal inventory we go down the left column writing the name of everyone we hold a resentment toward (column 1 in the chart below). There is no statute of limitations on resentment. It may be associated with events from the previous week or the second grade. If it pops up, trust that it has come up for a reason and write it down. When we have finished, we go back to the top of the page and list the reasons

---

[7] Matthew 5:23-24
[8] For further reading please see Alcoholics Anonymous' self-titled text, *Alcoholics Anonymous* and the companion text, *Twelve Steps and Twelve Traditions*
[9] "Richard Rohr's Daily Meditation": Sunday, June 15, 2014

we are resentful, how the situation has affected us, our part in the resentment, and the motivating fear (columns 2-5).

Column 1: I am resentful at: (name of person, place, or thing)	Column 2: Because they: (the reason)	Column 3: How does this affect me? (the effects of the previous column)	Column 4: My Part: (What have I done to create the historical situation, the resentment, or both: where have I been selfish, dishonest, or inconsiderate?)	Column 5: I am afraid of: (What fear motivated this behavior?)
1) Tony (my boss)	He cut me off in the meeting. He interrupts and makes the whole thing about him and what he thinks.	Confidence, personal/ sexual relations, ambition, self-esteem, personal security, etc	I do not assert myself and finish what I have to say. I will not let go of it. I play the victim role.	I am afraid that I am not smart enough or that I have nothing of value to say. Holding onto the resentment excuses me from sharing my opinions.
2) Mom	She ran over my bike	(use examples above or add your own)	I left the bike behind her car. I thought the bike enabled me to fit in.	I'm still afraid I'm not 'cool' enough. I still think I need external objects to vouch for me...just not bikes but cars, clothes, etc.

It is no accident that the chart above offers little room to manipulate the truth. The inventory is ours, not the other person's. "Though a situation had not been entirely our fault," writes Wilson, "we tried to disregard the other person involved entirely. Where were we to blame? Where were we selfish, dishonest, self-seeking and frightened? When we saw our faults we listed them. We placed them before us in black and white."[10]

---

[10] Bill Wilson, *Alcoholics Anonymous*, Alcoholics Anonymous World Services (2001), pg. 67

It is important that we not allow our momentum to fizzle out. This is a heavy practice. It is easy to procrastinate as the discomfort builds, so we should set our minds to the work and complete the task before us. Devote at least an hour to this process every day until the inventory is completed. This should not take more than two weeks. If you have trouble getting started, begin with an easy one. Bring to mind someone you are mad at or disappointed in and ask, "Why am I upset with this person? How does this resentment affect me? What is my part in the resentment? What fear is motivating my part in the resentment?"

Admission

Spiritual growth depends upon space. Self-analysis brings us into our hypocrisy where we discover room to grow. It exposes the gap between who we think we are and the life we are living.

The ability to see past what we think of ourselves to the life we're actually living is often the difference between progress and stagnation. When we defend our self-image, we defend the status quo. Growth cannot take place in a person who does not recognize room to grow within themselves. The recognition of hypocrisy is a sign of strength and hope, not weakness. It enables us to see where we stand and from there carve out a path that resonates with who we are on a deeper level.

Sometimes the confrontation with our hypocrisy challenges the sincerity and efficacy of our religious beliefs. We may consider ourselves spiritual people, but despite this consideration we are still plagued by fear, anger, stress, selfishness, and self-centeredness. When we allow our actions to do the talking, it becomes obvious that we do not practice many of principles we preach.

Confronting our hypocrisy is difficult. It requires that we "swallow and digest some big chunks of truth about ourselves," as Wilson put it.[11] These chunks of truth may be difficult to swallow, but it is important to remember that truth is self-liberating. When a liar admits he is lying, he ceases to be a liar. The moment we get honest with ourselves about our self-deception, humility sprouts. It is the practice of admission that brings about this transformation.

Immediately following our self-analysis we must share the findings with a spiritual friend.[12] Admission is a crucial part of the process. Our inventory shows us where we need to grow and admission enables us to step into the space. It is the mechanism by which we accept the findings of our inventory. When we read our inventory to another person, it brings it into focus for us.

Sharing our inventory with another person is not about getting something off of our chest. Self-analysis is not an external movement. It is a turn within. Just as a carnival ticket that reads "Admit One" permits us to get on the ride, the practice of admission permits self-knowledge to penetrate our mind-stream and affect change. Admission is the act of acceptance that "digests" those uncomfortable "chunks of truth." But self-knowledge alone is incapable of affecting sustainable change. This knowledge must be cultivated. It must be transformed into action.

---

[11] Bill Wilson, *Alcoholics Anonymous*, Alcoholics Anonymous World Services (2001), pg. 71

[12] This person can be a priest, minister, rabbi, spiritual teacher, or mentor. If you do not have a spiritual advisor, you can share your inventory with an understanding friend. If they are interested, lend them your copy of this book and let them go through the process as well.

Internal Restitution

Self-knowledge is transformed into action through internal restitution. Restitution is a change to the inner-workings of our mind. It uproots the distorted motivations of the false-self system, called in Steps Six and Seven of Alcoholics Anonymous, "defects of character" and "shortcomings." These defects are scars on our character. They are our natural instincts, mangled and distorted by the false-self system and its ravenous search for validation, reputation, and material success.

The false-self is false, so it cannot create. Instead it distorts and redirects the flow of our instinctual energies toward the fruition of its agenda. The false-self repurposes our human instincts: love is transformed into lust, creativity into busyness, gratitude into gluttony, pride into self-righteousness, and peace into laziness. The process of restitution heals these wounds and restores our original character.

In religious lingo, restitution is referred to as "repentance." Repentance is a change in direction. Jesus said, "Repent, for the Kingdom of Heaven is at hand." This does not mean, "Quick! Apologize or God is going to get you!" This "naughty or nice" mentality bears more resemblance to Christmas than spirituality. Just as an amendment to the U.S. Constitution is a fundamental change in the document, to repent is to change the direction of our search for happiness.

Repentance means turn around because the causes of happiness are within. We need to search ourselves, rather than the external world. When we drive all blame into ourselves and assume responsibility for our life, we make a fundamental change in our orientation toward the world. We set this ball in motion with our personal inventory. Now we must take it one step further. We must uproot the underlying motivations of the false-self system—the defects of character themselves, which take us out of ourselves in search of happiness.

We review our inventory, looking at columns four and five to see where we were selfish, greedy, dishonest, angry, inconsiderate, or afraid. If our past behavior was dishonest—infidelity, lying, theft, or pretentiousness—restitution is a change that addresses dishonesty in general, not just the specific examples of dishonesty listed. The specific examples are addressed in the next step. Here we are concerned with the principal issue. We are letting go of the milder manifestations of our shortcomings, not just the few that have proven injurious to us in the past. This means we are giving up the whole gamut of dishonesty—everything from lying by omission to marital infidelity. Often times, this brings us face-to-face with yet another uncomfortable truth about ourselves.

Most of us are willing to part ways with our more extreme shortcomings. But if we are honest, we will have to admit that we find comfort in their milder manifestations. Perhaps we are willing to part ways with the rage that drives us to physical violence or erratic outbursts. But are we willing to let go of the milder examples that casually belittle others to make us feel superior? "Isn't it true," asks Bill Wilson, "that we like to let greed masquerade as ambition?" Do we pretend to be something we're not because it's easier to fit in than it is to be true to our Self? Is pretending to be someone we are not any less dishonest than a flat out lie? Both are a deviation from the truth, and a shortcoming is any behavior that "falls short" of our True Nature. The spiritual imperative to be true to our Self dictates that we live by the maxim, "A half truth is a whole lie."

Internal restitution is about letting go of the defects of character that underlie the entire spectrum of selfish behavior—from the mild to the extreme. We cultivate this resolve by silently reflecting on the harm done to ourselves and others by even the more tempered examples of our shortcomings. When we let greed masquerade as ambition does our self-worth fluctuate with every success and failure? Does it cut into the time we need to take care of ourselves? Does it prevent us from spending quality time with our family? Do we have the right to deprive our children of needed love and attention? When we allow self-righteous anger to belittle others, are we left feeling superior or do we feel disgust and regret? When we pretend to be something we are not, does it elevate our self-esteem or are we left feeling fake and inauthentic? These are the types of questions we have to ask ourselves. And more importantly, we must listen to the answers.

Once we understand the consequences of our shortcomings, we can cultivate a resolve to let go of these patterns of consciousness and behavior. Notice I said "let go," not "overcome." We are not fighting against our shortcomings or waging a spiritual war. We bind ourselves to what we battle. Instead of waging a war, we are cultivating awareness and intent. We want to see these self-defeating patterns for what they are: self-defeating. When we see them as self-defeating, revulsion arises of its own accord. As our awareness deepens, so will our resolve.

We pray past our shortcomings. Moving down our list, we pray for the "strength and courage to be true to our Self" in the face of fear, anger, dishonesty, arrogance, jealousy, busyness, and self-pity. We allow each word of the prayer to be absorbed. We continue in this way until we have prayed for every identified shortcoming. The formal period of internal restitution should be conducted immediately after sharing your inventory with your spiritual friend and should last about an hour.

Making Amends

A proper amendment is not limited to our inner life. We cannot hang out within the cozy confines of an introverted spirituality. That leads to narcissism and introversion. We have to work with the suffering in the world, and that begins with the suffering we have created. The final stage of reconciliation in the program of Alcoholics Anonymous is the Ninth Step which reads, "Made direct amends to such people (those we have harmed) wherever possible, except when to do so would injure them or others."

We are careful never to make "direct amends" without first completing the process of restitution. But, we must be just as careful not to stop with internal restitution. If our internal work does not produce external fruits, then our internal work is self-delusion. Action authenticates spirituality. Without action it is wishful thinking, not spiritual practice.

We have to go back and make amends for the harm we have caused. To begin, we compile a list of persons we have harmed. This shouldn't take long. Many of the names will be on our personal inventory. Then, we say a prayer for each person on that list every morning for one week. If there is resistance, we extend the prayers for that person beyond the allotted week. We pray for them every day until the resistance falls away. We can use the prayer below or another prayer that embodies similar principles:

> (**Name of the person**), *I want you to be free of suffering.*
>
> (**Name of the person**), *I want you to be happy.*
>
> (**Name of the person**), *May peace be with you.*

When we have completed our prayer list, we return to the persons we have harmed and admit our wrong-doings directly to them. Most often, the people closest to us are the ones we have hurt the most. We are quick to project our troubles onto them, burdening them with our pain and fear. We go to them and ask what we can do to make it right and remain willing to follow through with their requests. Then we move down our list, returning to each individual we have harmed to make direct amends.

We are not there to preach. As St. Francis said, "Preach the gospel, and if necessary, use words." It is about action. If we owe them money, then we repay them; that is the nature of our sermon. We must be careful not to defend ourselves. To apologize is "to defend." Just as the discipline of apologetics seeks to defend a particular position, our apologies defend our behavior. Obviously, we may express remorse by saying "I'm sorry," but this should be followed up by action.

Under no circumstances should we try to justify ourselves. The words "I'm sorry, *but…*" should never come out of our mouth. The word "but" is an attempt to deflect responsibility. Nor should we retaliate, if the person in question is still hurt and refuses to hear us out. We give them the time and space they need to come to terms with whatever harm we have done to them. There may be instances where the other person involved becomes aggressive or abusive. We should not expose ourselves to abuse, whether it be emotional, verbal, or physical. We should remind ourselves of the part we have played in this unfortunate situation and remove ourselves without retaliating.

The ninth step of Alcoholics Anonymous does have one caveat: "except when to do so would injure them or others." If someone would be harmed by our admission, then we withhold it. If the other person is unaware of our offense and would not benefit from our admission, we have no choice but to keep it to our self. We are careful not to harm innocent bystanders either. If a confession would injure our family or the other person's family, then we must take an indirect route. When a direct amends is not possible, indirect amends are our only option. In such cases, we vow never to treat another person that way and to do the necessary work to maintain that vow. These vows bind our inner and outer work together.

The Path Forward

Every novice takes vows when initiated into a religious community. The vows we take are extracted from the process of self-analysis. They are not prefabricated vows, but personal resolutions born out of a sincere desire to move beyond our shortcomings. William Blake said, "The fool who persists in his folly will become wise." The wisdom of our vows is born out of our folly. We acknowledge where we have fallen short. Out of this awareness emerges a path that connects our inner world with the world of our responsibilities. We vow to walk this path. This is an individualistic approach, which is typical of Western spirituality. The renowned mythologist Joseph Campbell captures the individualistic spirit of Western spirituality with this tale from Arthurian legend:

> *"Sir Gawain, (King) Arthur's nephew, proposes a vow, since they thought it a disgrace to go forth in a group, each should enter the forest at that point where he found it darkest, and where no other path existed. This is the absolute opposite to the Oriental guru system, in which you accept the direction of a guru who knows what is best for you. But it is you and your potential character, which has never been seen and which can be brought into being by no one else, that is the life quest in the Western sense. Each individual pursues it in his or her own way."* [13]

Where there was no path, suddenly a path emerges. This path emerges from our self-analysis. We identify our shortcomings and enter ourselves at the darkest point. When we notice the gulf that separates who we are and the life we are living, we step into that space. We vow to bind the truth of our conscience with the outer world of our responsibilities. This vow brings us onto our path, but a vow without action is an empty promise. A proper vow brings our intentions and actions together. If we struggle with anger, for example, we vow not to lash out, but we must also vow to pray for those we resent on a daily basis.

While this concludes the exhaustive form of self-analysis, we must continue to take personal inventory on a daily basis. So we will now turn our attention to the condensed form of self-analysis, journaling.

---

[13] Joseph Campbell, *Thou Art That: Transforming Religious Metaphor,* New World Library (2001), pg. 30

The Practice of Journaling

Journaling is a regular practice. It is perhaps the most practical form of self-analysis because we can practice it every morning or every evening. However, journaling is not a substitute for the more exhaustive form of self-analysis outlined above. It is a condensed form of self-analysis that we can practice daily, which enables us to maintain a clear conscience and steady growth. Through consistent practice, self-awareness becomes a working part of the mind.

Once again, the main point involved is honesty. When journaling is spontaneous, it is honest. We are not writing for an audience, not even an internal one. We need to speak candidly with ourselves. Stream of consciousness journaling is a great way to practice self-honesty. The unbridled flow of consciousness pulls us past the censor, allowing us to put to paper whatever rises to the surface of our mind.

Self-analysis is *not* psycho-analysis. We are not trying to diagnose ourselves. We are following the trail of crumbs left in the wake of our exodus from the body. Self-analysis tells a story—the story of how we alienated ourselves from our True Life. This story hitches itself to our awareness which is often trapped on the outer edges of our life and brings us back to our center. In this sense, journaling is like the meditative practice taught by Carl Jung called Active Imagination. Journaling the stream of consciousness is more than a writing exercise. It is prayer.

***

To begin the practice, find a comfortable seat and bring your awareness to the tip of the nose. Feel the coolness of the inhalation and the warmth of the exhalation. Feel your butt in the chair. Sit in this way for a minute or two. Then ask for a topic. Just sit and wait for a topic, theme, or question to arise. Once you have it, write it at the top of the page and begin journaling. If you are struggling to find a topic try, "If my heart could speak, what would it say?" or "Where have I fallen short?" Open ended topics leave room for exploration.

We are not looking for a philosophical rant. Remember, there isn't an audience to impress. We are looking for honesty. Write for ten minutes. Do not pick your pen up from the paper until the ten minutes has expired. Just write. If you are stuck or at a loss for words, rewrite the topic where your pen sits. It does not matter how ridiculous or off topic it appears to be, just write.

A clear conscience is a prerequisite for contemplative practice. You cannot come to the altar when you are not right with your fellow man.[14] You can't get to the altar because the pathways are clogged. An honest examination of ourselves unclogs the pathway between the mind and heart. The forms of self-analysis above represent a panoramic approach toward the purification of our conscience. They expose the gap between our True Self and the life we are living.

Now we will take a closer look at the false-self image and the backdrop of impermanence upon which it is projected.

---

[14] Matthew 12:23-24

3 THE BACKDROP OF IMPERMANENCE

> *When asked to sum up the Buddha's teachings in one phrase, Suzuki Roshi said, "Everything changes."* [1]

The underlying cause of our discontentment is the belief in a solid, separate self. But context is crucial to our understanding of the false-self. Why is our belief in a solid, separate self a false belief? To answer this question we will need to turn our attention toward the backdrop upon which the false-self is projected—the backdrop of impermanence.

We have all heard about impermanence. It has become a threadbare spiritual catchword, along with its sterile cousin, "the present moment." Intellectually we understand the concept of impermanence but we do not feel it. This detached knowledge fails to effect change. The intent here is not to explain the concept of impermanence, but to point it out—to wake you up to the truth of impermanence within yourself.

Impermanence is a fact. The Greek philosopher Heraclitus famously said, "No same man could walk through the same river

---

[1] Nalanda Translation Committee, "The Four Reminders," www.nalandatranslation.org

twice because the man and the river have since changed." Impermanence is the nature of life and all that lives. In fact, change is just another word for living—"to live" means "to grow" and growth is change. But few of us are conscious of this fact, which means we go through life without living fully.

Life is the blossoming of our inmost nature and living is our conscious participation in that process. To participate we must be present. The false-self is assembled with thought and thought flows forth from memory. "We have no transition from one imagination to another," writes Thomas Hobbes, "whereof we never had the like before in our senses."[2] Simply put, we don't think about it unless we have experienced it—or some variation thereof.

Memory is formed from sense impressions and, through a process of association called "thinking," it is recollected. In other words, thinking is memory set in motion. Consequently, when we identity with thought, we experience ourselves as something that has already happened. We see ourselves as a finished product, and to be done is to be dead. The false-self is a thought-self, an image created and maintained by the thinking mind. So when we identify with the false-self, we feel dead inside.

The Apple Doesn't Fall Far From the Tree

The natural world is not *in* a constant state of fluctuation. It *is* fluctuation. The natural world is forever growing, evolving, disintegrating, dying, and giving birth to new life. Furthermore, we are not born *into* this world. We are born out of it. Mankind

---

[2] Thomas Hobbes, *Leviathan* (Hackett Publishing Company 1994), pg. 12

is a product of nature. We grow out of the earth just like a dandelion, apple, or a pine tree. Since we come from nature, our nature is change—or better yet, our True Nature is the space or plasticity that facilitates birth, growth, adaptation, disintegration, and death. In short, the apple does not fall far from the tree.

Our True Self is a process of unfolding, not a solid entity. We are not a noun, but a verb. When we think of ourselves as a solid, permanent entity we separate ourselves from nature, which lives within us as our True Nature. This is the inner meaning of "exile" in the Jewish tradition. The concept of spiritual exile comes from the Hebrew word *galut*, which, according to Nobel Laureate Elie Wiesel, means "everything is moving except me."[3]

The Song of Life

Alan Watts, the popular philosopher of Eastern religion, used to compare life to music. "The point of music is music," he would say. People enjoy listening to music for the rhythm, the stream of melody. No one listens to music to hear it end. If they did, as Watts pointed out, their favorite songs would be the ones that began and ended with a single uproar of noise. Life is the same way. The point of life is to live, to participate in the melody. Melodies are streams; they are flowing. You cannot freeze them. When you do, there is no flow. That is spiritual death.

The only way to participate in the melody is through basic awareness. Basic awareness is open. It is fluid. An open mind loses its sense of self in the music, whereas a self-centered mind tries to pause the song. It is not enough to enjoy the music. The

---

[3] Elie Wiesel, "We Are All Witnesses," *The Inner Journey: Views from the Jewish Tradition*, Morning Light Press (2007), pg. 302

self-centered mind wants to know the words. It wants to identify with the song. So the false-self rewinds it, trying to commit the lyrics to memory and claim the song as its own.

The false-self derives a sense of identity or meaning from its interactions with "other." These interactions produce vouchers—memories or impressions that we collect and try to redeem at a later date for validation. The false-self isn't concerned with being there, but what being there says about it. Instead of enjoying the concert, the false-self takes pictures of the show to prove it was there. It is more focused on making a mental scrapbook than participating in the experience.

The false-self is the ultimate hoarder—it keeps every voucher, every memory from which it stands to profit. A self-centered mind is a cluttered mind. There is no space, no room to breathe. Deep down the false-self knows that at any moment its whole world could collapse. It remembers the space at our core—the silent gap between each note that enables the song of life to flow. This memory haunts the false-self. It breeds paranoia and insecurity because it challenges the solidity of the false-self. The silence between each note reminds us that everything changes, including the self.

Everything Changes

Things change. But the river isn't the only thing that changes. According to Heraclitus, so does the man. Unfortunately, the false-self doesn't see it that way. It sees itself as unchanging. When we stand in the river of life with our feet planted in the ground, life feels overwhelming. Daily life feels like a wall of water bearing down on us. Take, for example, the transition from being single to in a relationship.

When you are single, you develop a lifestyle that doesn't have to take another person into consideration. You can wake up, drink your coffee, listen to music, have breakfast, go to work, stop by the gym afterwards, hang out with friends, and watch whatever you want on television. But when you bring another person into the mix, you cannot go on living as if they aren't there. The situation has changed, so your old schedule and your old self-image are outdated. When "I" is a fixed entity or a habit of thought, this transition is difficult. When you cling to the expired image, the relationship feels claustrophobic, like there isn't enough space for the other person. There is one confrontation after the other. The intensity continues to build over time until everything—your self-image and the relationship—washes out.

What we think about ourselves is challenged by change. Spiritual practice is our response to this challenge. Many people say, "I shouldn't have to change to be in a relationship." I say, if you don't change, then you aren't in a relationship. In fact, if you don't give up who you are every day, then you are not living. To be alive is to be in a constant state of revolution. Changing situations *should* affect our behavior. That is sanity. Confucius said, "They who would abide in wisdom must often change." A sane mind is a renewed mind inspired by emerging information. Our point of view—the man in Heraclitus's example—must remain open or fluid. The ego has to be transparent to our experience.

"Everything changes," is the basic point, according to Shunryu Suzuki. Everything—society, politics, the weather, relationships, our beliefs, and the physical body—is fluctuating. When we are open to change, the transition is relatively smooth. For example, we can easily adapt our diet to the changing demands of our aging body, if we are open and receptive. When we allow our bachelor lifestyle to be swept away by the tide of impermanence, we realize there is plenty of space for our new partner. On the other hand, when we try to save our vouchers, we drown. We cannot swim when our hands are full.

In basic awareness, the man and the river pour into one another. Things change and this change is so pervasive, so continuous, that you cannot determine where one thing begins and the other ends. The line between the man and the river is blurred. At this point, the truth of impermanence deepens. It transforms into the truth of selflessness.

Life is change. Change is life. They are the same thing. Trying to organize impermanent phenomena into permanent categories of thought is a frustrating and impossible waste of energy. It is like trying to herd cats. Furthermore, we are not other than this change—we are life. We are change. The river of life flows through our core, emptying out into the truth of selflessness. We are not a noun standing on the bank watching life flow by; we are a verb or a wave emerging out of the stream of impermanence.

Now we will turn our attention toward the false-self system and the truth of selflessness.

4 THE BIRTH OF THE FALSE-SELF

> *"All the harm with which this world is rife,*
> *all fear and suffering that there is, clinging*
> *to the 'I' has caused it!"* ~ *Shantideva* [1]

The human journey is the unfolding of our person into the field of time and space. Spiritual practice is the vehicle that enables us to make the journey. However, the spiritual path is not a self-existing phenomenon. Spirituality is man-made. The spiritual path co-emerges with the path that gives rise to suffering. Every time we resist the life preordained by our True Nature to become who or what we *think* we *should* be, we leave a path in our wake. This trail of crumbs is the spiritual path.

The path of suffering and the spiritual path are two movements along one line. Steps 1, 2, 3, 4, 5 take us out of ourselves, and steps 5, 4, 3, 2, and 1 bring us back. Travelling out from the center toward the perimeter is the path of suffering; moving from the perimeter back toward the center is spirituality. Since the road to suffering is carved out by willful acts of Self-rejection, the spiritual path is paved with radical acts of Self-acceptance. Willfulness pushes us down the path of suffering; acceptance reconnects us with the life of the body.

---

[1] Shantideva, *The Bodhisattva's Guide to the Way of Life,* Shambala (2006), pg. 127

Acceptance is not some vague platitude; it is the thrust behind all spiritual practice. Acceptance is the act of consent that transcends those willful patterns of thought and behavior that suppress our True Self, enabling the inner world of our potentialities to pour into the world of action and responsibility.

False-self vs. True Self

The terms "false-self" and "True Self" can be vague. So what is meant by each? The ego is a conceptual overlay held above the light of our emerging life and projected outward. It is natural and useful. The ego is a proxy or a surrogate self, so to speak. It enables us to navigate the conventional world—to show up at work on time, safely negotiate rush hour traffic, or meet a friend for coffee. The ego becomes a false-self when we misidentify with the projection. When we mistake the external image for our real self, it becomes a false-self.

The false-self is self-conscious. It is an external image, so it constantly thinks about how it is perceived by others. Through repetition, this self-referencing state of mind becomes a habit. As a result, we get stuck in our head. The false-self is a habit of thought. Since habit is not our original nature but something extra, we might call the false-self our second nature.

Habits are fixed or predetermined. They are a form of memory—reenactments of previous behaviors and states of consciousness. The false-self is an amalgamation of memories stitched together by discursive thought. Like a shadow puppet, this aggregated image is held over the light of the present moment, creating the illusion of life. Of course, the illusion of life is no substitute for our True Life, so any life identified with a false-self will be unsatisfactory.

The True Self is not a static entity. It is Being beyond name and form. In this sense, *Being* does not refer to "a being that stands apart from other beings." When I speak of "Being" (with a capital B), I mean "undifferentiated or unconscious awareness." In undifferentiated awareness there is no division between mind and body. Inspiration and action (emptiness and form), are Cartesian points plotted along the ever-expanding axis that is our life. This life or Self, if you will, is a process, not an event. It is the ceaseless percolation of our Being that carries our inmost potential into the field of action.

Formlessness is vibrant. It is not dead space or nothingness. It is *no-thing-ness*. This no-thingness is the space that enables our life to flow. Without space there is no room for growth, so formlessness is the truth of selflessness that begets life. It is the plasticity that permits us to pass through the stages of human maturation.

"When we abandon the idea that what we 'really' are is a centralized self corresponding to our ideas, we discover ourselves as the unceasing, ever-changing kaleidoscope of experience that arises as our life," writes Dr. Reginald Ray. "So we discover that we are, in each moment, a truly individual phenomenon, not limited even (or especially) by any notion of a continuous or coherent self. . . . We begin to realize, in other words, that our life is ultimately not a personal phenomena at all."[2] In short, our life is both impersonal and individual. The True Self is selfless.

Language and the False-self

If the belief in a solid-separate self is false, then why does

---

[2] Dr. Reginald Ray, *Touching Enlightenment: Finding Realization in the Body*, Sounds True (2008) pg. 173

everyone experience it as if it were real? The answer is illusion. As a species, our strength is found in numbers. For all the war and bloodshed brought about by the human race, our survival as a species is owed to our ability to commune. Nature has equipped us with tools capable of transforming an "I" and a "you" into a "we."

It is our nature to commune, so we generate *forms* that represent the *formlessness* of our inner life and birth them into the world. These forms are symbols. Language is a system of symbols that translates the incommunicable nature of our formless experience into a metaphorical language that is intelligible to others. When we press our point of view out into the world of time and space and others relate, our first and second person singular perspectives (I/you) are transformed into first person plural (we).

Communication enables us to find commonality with others. There is virtually an absolute separation between "I" and "you" when we first meet. Then, in the course of conversation we find *common* ground—perhaps we like the same football team or support the same political candidate. At this point, the distinction between "I" and "you" is *converted* into "we."

Relationship is about intimacy. It begins with giving shape to our inner world. We express ourselves by generating words, images, and gestures that point past themselves back to the truth in our heart. In this way, our inner life is pressed out or articulated. Through the process of articulation, inspiration becomes an artifact—a form that represents our inner-life.

Unfortunately, we become obsessed with our artifacts. We cling to our past works of art, instead of returning to the creative process. We mistake the symbol for the experience it was intended to express and as a result find ourselves alienated from the source of life. No artifact is treasured more than the word "I." That little word is, as Shantideva states in the opening quotation, the cause of all our fear and suffering. It is both the inceptive cause and the most frequent instigator of the destructive mental glitch commonly referred to as self-centeredness. Why does this happen?

Mistaking the Map for the Territory

The word "I" is devoid of symbolic value. It is incapable of pointing past itself. It always refers to that which made the reference. "The referencer," so to speak, is thought. So "I" is a glitch in the system that creates a self-conscious loop. It causes us to think about our own thoughts. When we think about our own thoughts, we create the illusion of solidity. The fog of thought becomes so thick that it is hard to tell the difference between what we think and reality. As a result, we mistake our self-image for the genuine article.

Just as a picture book generates the illusion of a moving picture when the pages are turned rapidly, the musings of our mind appear to be real when we anxiously think about our own thoughts. This inbred pattern of thought becomes habitual through repetition and self-centeredness is installed as our second nature or default mode of consciousness. This habitual identification with "I" locates the sense of self at the level of the thinking mind and transforms the unformed awareness of the body into "other," severing the mind's link to the real world.

The sounds, smells, sights, tastes, and textures that make up the present moment find expression in the basic awareness of the body. When the mind separates itself from the body, it cuts itself off from the energy of reality. When we alienate ourselves from the present moment, life becomes "other than." It becomes something "out there"—some "thing" we do rather than the essence of who we are. This leaves us feeling lifeless.

A disembodied mind has no life. It has no world, so it has to create one. It has to think a new world into existence. This turns life into a possession which implies an owner. The real world is replaced by *our* world and sanity is lost. Initially, the relationship between the mind and body was only fractured, now it is restructured. Reality is now under the dominion of the thinking mind, which means our point of view is no longer shaped by reality, but instead by the previous thought. This is insanity.

Insanity is a point of view disconnected from the basic awareness of the body. This disembodied state of mind is unaccountable to reality. It is a hallucinated world, created and maintained by inbred thought. Enthroned at the center, as the creator and lord of this new world, is "I." It is the metric that determines the value and worth of everyone and everything in its environment.

A disembodied mind is a self-centered mind. Self-centeredness does not see people, places, and things as they are. It only sees their utility or how they affect us. If they make us feel warm and fuzzy, we call them a friend and cling to them. If they threaten us, we label them an asshole and treat them as such. They are not seen from their side. Self-centeredness only sees them from our side. "I" only sees what it thinks, the map. It is detached from the territory.

Earth is just earth when seen from outer-space. There is no Alabama, Canada, or China. Similarly, when seen from inner-space, life is as-it-is. There is no elaboration. There are no boundaries separating self and other, friend and enemy. The thinking mind adds the lines. The lines are not a problem, unless we take them too seriously. When we cling to them, we draft new maps based not on the territory, but on previous maps. We make maps of our maps or think about our own thoughts until our world-view is shaped more by our self-centered imagination than reality.

The Spectrum of Awareness

In truth, the map belongs to the territory. Thought is a function of the body. The mind and body are not separate when seen from inner-space. This is how a child sees the world. At birth we are embodied. We may not be very coordinated, but before language there is no basis for differentiation. So, there is no division between mind and body or self and the environment.

It is true that children intuit oneness, but undifferentiated awareness is not consigned to the early stages of our development. It is not infantile awareness, but fundamental awareness. As adults, it still lives within us as primary awareness. And from time to time, it pops out from behind the clouds: spiritual experiences, near-death experiences, and moments of awe. In depth psychology this is called the "oceanic feeling."

Spiritual experiences are troubling for materialists. They label them wishful thinking, deny them, or write them off as regressions into an earlier state of consciousness. But spiritual experiences cannot be dismissed so easily. They are a universal phenomenon. Even the most passionate atheist would have to admit to having transcendent experiences that might be labeled "spiritual," though they would likely choose another word.

Spiritual experiences are problematic only when the

inherence of the false-self is tacitly accepted. When the mind-body division is taken as real, the oceanic feeling appears to be a recollection of infantile consciousness. But when the sense of self is regarded as a figment of our imagination, the oceanic feeling is not problematic. It is a flash of undifferentiated awareness breaking through the clouds of dualistic thinking.

In *Varieties of Religious Experience,* William James wrote, 'Our normal waking consciousness, rational consciousness as we call it, is but one special type of consciousness, whilst all about it, parted from it by the filmiest of screens, there lie potential forms of consciousness entirely different."[3] This is consistent with Buddhist psychology which, as Traleg Kyabgon Rinpoche explains, "acknowledges a structural formation of self-identity, with many different types of identification based on various levels of consciousness and distinctive levels of being, but it doesn't endorse a separately existing self."[4] The default state of consciousness (waking or rational) is but one form of consciousness; beneath it there are more fundamental states of awareness.

When we identify solely with "our normal waking consciousness," we are cut off from the depths of our Being. The tendency to think about our own thoughts casts shade on the spectrum of awareness. It blots out most of who we are, leaving us identified with a sliver of our life. We substitute the lived experience of life for what we think about life. This is like eating a cookbook for dinner. Disembodiment alienates us from life, but there is a marked difference between alienation and extinction.

---

[3] William James, *Varieties of Religious Experience*, The New American Library (1964), pg. 298
[4] Traleg Kyabgon, *The Practice of Lojong,* Shambhala (2007), pg. 91

The Call of Silence

Our True Life has not been snuffed out. We are just ignoreant of it. If we tune out the noise of insanity, we can still hear our heart calling to us from beyond the veil. This call is at the core of all sincere religion. But this call haunts us because we do not know how to respond. We anticipate the Ground of Being and its vast potential, but we have forgotten how to access it. We try to investigate transrational forms of consciousness with the only tool at our immediate disposal, thought. In the famous words of Albert Einstein, "We cannot solve our problems with the same thinking we used when we created them." When we attempt to think our way out of thinking, we find that we are just thinking about not thinking.

We try to solve the problem with the same strategy we used to create it because we know of no other way. Our inability to move beyond the veil leads to the mistaken belief that we are stuck in this disembodied state. Therefore, we feel hopeless.

In reality, we are not stuck between our ears. Rational consciousness is not the fundamental mode of consciousness. It is the default mode. There are more fundamental forms of awareness beneath the surface. The intellect must be accountable to these primary modes of awareness. Much like a map exists in relationship to its territory, rational consciousness must work with the *Isness* of the present moment as reflected by basic awareness. As the terrain changes, so must the map, which means the ego must remain open and receptive to the emerging life of the body. The ego is neither the Alpha nor the Omega. It is an intermediary. It mediates the relationship between the unconscious depths of the body and the field of our incarnation.

A healthy ego understands its role. It sees itself as a proxy sent into the world to do the bidding of our heart. There is nothing wrong with having an ego. "It is quite true," writes Kyabgon Rinpoche, "that in the relative world we cannot just casually get rid of our ego, for the ego is a vital part of us that has a function."[5] We need a healthy ego to live in the relative world. However, a healthy ego is transparent. To borrow the words of Thomas Merton, a healthy ego is like a clean window. As it receives the light of reality, more of the light is seen and less of the window. A healthy ego knows it's *only* one level of identification, not *the* only level. When we mistake the ego for the source of light, it is installed as a false-self. The false-self does not know it's an agent. It *thinks* it is the principal.

Conclusion

The notion of a solid or independently existing self ignores the interdependent relationship between direct experience and thought. The alternate realities proposed by the self-centered mind have no ontological ground, apart from the experiential fact that thoughts exist as physiological phenomena arising within the envelope of skin. They exist as sensations within the body, but not as superimposed realities.

"First thought, best thought," Trungpa Rinpoche used to say. It is inspired thought, but the second thought is second guessing, and with each successive thought we remove ourselves from the precision and freshness of the present moment. One thought arises. We think about that thought, and then we're two thoughts removed. We continue on in this way, thinking about each of the previous thoughts, until we are hundreds of thoughts removed from the present moment. This is how *we deviate from the*

---

[5] Traleg Kyabgon, *The Practice of Lojong,* Shambhala (2007), pg. 95

journey preordained by our human nature. This is the path of suffering.

The spiritual path is the mind's return to the naked awareness of the body. It is the inverse of the path that gives rise to disembodiment. If steps 1, 2, 3, 4, and 5 produce suffering, then steps 5, 4, 3, 2, and 1 bring us back to the body. Practice encourages us to let go of the false-self system so we may reconnect with the vastness and the immediacy of the body. It is about dropping the narrative, relaxing the tension, and taking refuge in our True Life.

5 PROJECT BECOMING

"We must be willing to let go of the life we planned so as to have the life that is waiting for us." ~ Joseph Campbell

The false-self might be a counterfeit but it feels real. The mind creates the appearance of solidity by thinking about its own thoughts until it obscures our view of reality. Fortunately, there are gaps between each of these thoughts. These gaps represent the possibility of freedom. They are breaks in the clouds—moments of clarity—through which the light of our True Life shines. These spiritual experiences remind us that, beyond the cloud cover, the luminous life of the body still burns bright.

Unfortunately, we are identified with the false-self and from the false-self's vantage point these gaps appear to be weaknesses. The false-self is weary of basic awareness. So we remain estranged from the body, which perpetuates our sense of inadequacy: "I am not good enough, strong enough, or smart enough." This poverty mentality turns our life into a brutal process of becoming—the obsessive pursuit of an antidotal outcome. There is always something big just around the corner and when we acquire it, we will have arrived, or so we believe.

Make no mistake about it; we are *always* becoming. In fact, becoming is our natural condition. Becoming is the movement of Being from potentiality to actuality. The violent process to which I am referring occurs when the false-self inserts a particular destination. Rather than taking the process of becoming as the point, a final point is installed. This end point is *the* point; it is the meaning of life, as far as the false-self is concerned. It believes that the point of life is to arrive, not live. So the false-self anxiously anticipates the day it will win reputation, validation, and success. The stressful pursuit of this elusive goal is fueled by insecurity.

The Ego and Insecurity

The false-self is driven by insecurity—a sense of inferiority stemming from the belief that we are missing something. In fact, the false-self is an attempt to compensate for these perceived insufficiencies. It is trying to become what it believes is missing. So, an insecure mind is a busy mind. It is always on the lookout for that magical missing ingredient—the square peg for the square shaped hole in our soul, so to speak. It feverishly awaits the grand finale: graduation, the big career, financial success, retirement, marriage, divorce, the birth of our first child, and independence from our last. All the while we are overlooking the point of life, which is to live. As a result we feel lifeless, which just reinforces the belief that we are broken or missing something. So, we try harder, ad infinitum.

"We must know that we have been created for greater things," says Mother Teresa, "not just to be a number in the world, not just to go for diplomas and degrees, this work and that work. We have been created in order to love and to be loved." When we read this we say, "Aw, that's sweet," but in the back of our minds we're thinking, "Love and spirituality are nice, but success and accomplishment are what really matter." So we try to figure out what success looks like and bring that image to fruition, instead of being true to our Self.

The desire for a warm bath is suppressed by our obsession with finishing that last stack of paper work; our evening walk is pushed aside to make the next phone call; morning meditation is postponed so we can get a head start on the busy day before us. Rather than taking a break to read or journal, we prostitute our Self for the approval of our employer. And to make matters worse, this is all done with the best of intentions—with a "this is going to hurt me more than it hurts you" kind of attitude.

We are stuck in a rut and can't get out. The only tools we have are the ones that dug the rut in the first place, so we keep digging. Every phone call leads to more work. The next stack of paperwork drives our husband or wife even further away, which creates another problem that takes up space in our head. So, we put off meditation, yet again.

We intend to come back to ourselves as soon as everything calms down. We are running ourselves to death to create time for relaxation. Take a moment to consider the backwardness of this approach: to produce peace and calm we rely upon the causes of stress and anxiety. We are *chasing* stillness and *worrying* about peace of mind.

Many of us approach spirituality like a 401k: as soon as our finances are in order, our work is complete, and the children are happy, we plan on taking time for our Self. Unfortunately, things never settle down. Years go by and we remain stressed out and discontented. Busyness doesn't just go away. We may take a vacation or go on retreat, but if we do not regularly create and defend the space needed for our life to unfold, we will find the stress and anxiety of "project becoming" awaiting our return.

Hitting Bottom

We all want to be free, but believe that freedom is earned. We think we have to get our shit together before we can invest in our sanity. Sadly, our shit never comes together. Instead, we run ourselves into the ground trying to create and maintain our many selves.

Project becoming is painful. It carves us up and compartmentalizes our life. There isn't just one of us anymore: there is who we are at home, the persona we take to work, and the various faces we present to our friends and acquaintances. We have to manage them all so we bounce from one fiasco to the next. We stay in crisis management mode, on the verge of a nervous breakdown.

Interestingly enough, these crises can be our saving grace. Hitting rock bottom can bring about decisive change. The word "crisis" comes from the Greek word *krisis*, meaning "a turning point." A crisis is a crack in the false-self system, through which the light of our True Life shines. When the light breaks through, we start to wake up.

Busyness is unsustainable. We can't keep up with all the stress and paranoia, the insecurity, the people-pleasing behavior, or the endless barrage of tasks. Constantly having to defend the previous success and earn the next one wears us out. It brings us to a breaking point. This breaking point is rock bottom—there is no plan B or exit strategy. We cannot continue living this way. Rock bottom is a confrontation with suffering that brings about decisive change. It is a turning point.

We are exhausted, afraid, stressed out, frustrated, sad, and there is nowhere to escape. The violent path of becoming has run its course. In the midst of our despair, we see our insanity for what it is. This is the moment of clarity. The restoration of sanity begins with the recognition of insanity—crazy people do not know they are crazy!

Everything is Workable

Despair forces us to start where we are. Our life is out of control. We do not know where to start. As children, we got frustrated when we had to clean our room before going out to play. Our room was so disorganized that we despaired of ever cleaning it. After a while, we noticed that the chaos was manageable if we focused on one thing at a time. If we pick our toys up one at a time, we are outside in a flash. Similarly, our life is manageable, if we focus on one thing at a time. If we start where we are, our situation is workable.

Suffering brings us back to the here-and-now, a place we have not been for some time. There we recover simplicity. Our situation is revealed to be workable. It might be sad or painful, but it is workable. We hop in the shower, grab our journal, or read a book. We take the dog out for the walk we've been putting off. The basic quality of wakefulness re-emerges as an invitation to sit with the simplicity of our breath for a few minutes. Throughout the day, we return to the immediacy of the present moment by reconnecting with the breath. And we do all of this in the face of busyness because busyness doesn't just go away. It is there the whole time, tugging at the belief in our inadequacy.

We can hear the phone calls, paperwork, and emails calling us back to project becoming. This is the undercurrent of insecurity pushing the idea that we must earn, not only love and acceptance, but the right to be. It takes courage to keep sitting.

We cut through all the noise with a deep breath. We feel our feet on the ground, our heart beating. In the silence of the body, we can't hear the drumbeat of insecurity. In the body, we find refuge.

Our True Life cares nothing about the projects, plans, fears, or ambitions of the false-self. The life of the body is like a tree root breaking through the concrete of our busy, insecure mind.[1] The heart only cares about the process of unfolding that is our human journey. It is our responsibility to defend the space that facilitates this journey. It is our job to cut through the stress, anxiety, aggression, and depression and come back to our *Self* over and over again.

Spirituality does not begin with love and compassion for our fellow man. We can't give away what we do not have. Before we can love those around us, we have to cultivate an attitude of loving-kindness towards our Self. Before we can free the other prisoners, we have to step out of our jail cell.

The real enemy is in our head. We have to be on guard against the false-self's agenda by fiercely defending the silence from which our True Life emerges. Obviously, this includes a daily practice of self-analysis, prayer, and meditation. But we must also be willing to drop what we are doing and grab a bite to eat when we are hungry or go to bed when we are tired. The busyness, the fear, the insatiable search for validation—none of it is just going to go away. We have to cut through it. We have to take action. Action is the antidote to busyness.

A life of busyness is a life of hoarding vouchers that we hope to exchange at a later date for the right to be. We do not

---

[1] Jeremiah 20:7

have to earn that right. It is embedded in the human condition. It is an inalienable right. Life cannot be earned or accomplished; it is a gift. Gifts are accepted, not achieved, which is why acceptance is at the core of all spiritual practice. We accept the gift of Being by turning within and taking refuge in the body.

6 REFUGE

"To repent is not to take on afflictive penances like fasting, vigils, flagellation, or whatever else appeals to our generosity. It means to change the direction in which you are looking for happiness. That challenge goes to the root of the problem." ~ *Fr. Thomas Keating* [1]

In the body, we find the blueprint for life. Our True Nature is like a seed that blossoms into a meaningful way of life when nourished by an open and direct relationship with reality. Real happiness is the joy of surrendering to this inborn design for living. We will never know such happiness unless we give up project becoming and take refuge in our True Self.

Becoming a Refugee

Suffering is a symptom of insanity—a point of view disconnected from the present moment. Insanity puts the cart before the horse, or in this case, what we think in front of reality. Taking refuge restructures the mind-body relationship. It reinstates the basic awareness of the body as the principal and

---

[1] Fr. Thomas Keating, *Journey to the Center: A Lenten Passage* (The Crossroad Publishing Company, 1998), pg . 11

returns the intellect to its rightful state of agency. In this way, taking refuge restores sanity.

Refuge is a change of attitude. It is a shift from willfulness to willingness. The difference between willfulness and willingness is the difference between a life organized around a self-determined goal and a life piloted by the ongoing revelation of our inmost nature. Refuge isn't a practice that can be taught in steps or stages. It is a spontaneous reaction to suffering. A refugee is someone who flees their native environment to escape the dictates of an oppressive regime. For someone to pick up and leave everything they've ever known, conditions have to be unbearable. There has to be a sense of despair. We take refuge when we hit rock bottom.

When the false-self is seen as an oppressive force, the desire for freedom spontaneously emerges. This deep yearning for freedom is the spirit of renunciation. Renunciation doesn't mean selling all of our possessions and entering the monastery. Every time we return to the present moment we are practicing renunciation. When we return to the breath in meditation, we are practicing renunciation. Renunciation is about giving up "our version" of the world—letting go of what *we think*. As renunciants, we no longer have a world. We are refugees.

The New World

Motivated by suffering, we set out in search of a new world. This new world has to have promise. Most importantly, it has to be practical. We are weary of belief systems that are not supported by practice and common sense. We have been disappointed by one self-help diet after another. Therefore, we are not looking for *The Secret*, *A Course on Miracles*, or another catchy slogan. Our object of refuge has to be a new way of seeing and relating to the world and it has to be actionable. Fortunately, there is such a land.

There is a world beyond the anxious and stressful one with which we are so accustomed. It is a state of simplicity that transcends our neurotic fears, outrageous expectations, and petty squabbles. It's a world that doesn't revolve around us, so life doesn't feel like some terrible thing that is happening to us. In this new world we are neither the architect nor the foreman. We are not charged with the task of creating or maintaining this world, so it is free of busyness. Here, the purpose of life is life itself. We get to retire from the burdensome task of playing God and start living. This world is constantly being made anew, so every moment is a fresh start.

This is not a remote or isolated place. We do not have to trek across high mountain passes or set sail across shark-infested waters. In fact, it's closer to us than we can imagine. "Do not look here or there! For, behold, the kingdom of God is within you."[2]

This new world is the life of the body, the present moment. It has been here all along, but we were unaware of it because we were asleep. The confrontation with suffering has awoken us from our slumber and now the light of the present moment is shining in our eyes. It is breaking through the clouds of our self-centered mind and the life of the body is re-emerging. This is the dawn of the awakened heart. Taking refuge is learning to trust the wisdom of the body.

Refuge is an act of devotion. In this context, devotion is not about reliance upon an external deity. We are not going out

---

[2] Luke 17:21

of ourselves, but coming back to our Self. Lama Yeshe, one of the pioneers of Buddhism in the West, described refuge as "a process of turning inward that begins with the discovery of our own unlimited potential as human beings."[3] We are turning within and placing our trust in the design for living outlined by our inmost nature. When we take refuge we give up our plans and ambitions, our preconceived ideas and preordained responses, and become a disciple of the body.

Happiness is available to all because the heart of enlightenment is beating within each of us. This is the basis of spirituality. It is precisely because this potential lies in wait that spirituality is down-to-earth. It is the truth and immediacy of our inmost nature—combined with a course of action—that legitimizes spirituality. Refuge isn't about turning away from human nature toward something supernatural or other-worldly. It is a radical acceptance *of* the human condition.

The human condition lives in the body. When I speak of the body, I am not simply referring to flesh and bone. "The notion of the body as some dissectible thing has only limited applicability," writes the Buddhist philosopher Herbert Guenther. The experience of the body is richer and deeper than our superficial conception of it—"for the body as lived by me," Guenther continues, "is not an object among other objects but the center for the varied intentionalities of world experience, of vision, actions, and interests."[4]

In this book, the word "body" reaches past the skeletal

---

[3] Thubten Yeshe, Lecture "Refuge," Switzerland (1978), www.lamayeshe.com/article/refuge

[4] Herbert Guenther, *From Reductionism to Creativity: rDzogs-chen and the New Sciences of Mind*, Shambhala (1989), pg. 227

structure upon which flesh is heaped to the nucleus of our life where original awareness and the possibility of transcendence reside. Therefore, it is a dynamic word that refers not to a static structure, but to the three modes of Being: Undifferentiated Awareness, Basic Sanity, and Incarnation. In these modes of Being, we find refuge from bondage, confusion, and lifelessness. In the body, we discover freedom, clarity, and vitality.

Undifferentiated Awareness

The awareness of the body is undifferentiated. It is free of all the false-self additives. Undifferentiated Awareness is *nothingness* or open-mindedness. It is capable of seeing anything because it isn't filled with preconceived ideas, fears, or expectations. Undifferentiated Awareness is without beginning or end, and therefore devoid of a center. It is selfless awareness. And since Undifferentiated Awareness is impersonal, life doesn't feel like it is happening to us. Because it is without the division of self and other there is no friction or conflict. Furthermore, it is whole or complete—needing nothing and as a result, beyond discontentment.

Once again, we need not exert any effort to produce unformed awareness. It is fundamental. Taking refuge in Undifferentiated Awareness is not about creating a new, state of the art enlightened mind. It is Original Mind. When we let go of what we think and relax into the silence of the body, we reconnect with Undifferentiated Awareness.

Basic Sanity

Selfless awareness is the abyss that says, "Let there be

light."[5] This light is Truth. Truth (with a capital T) is not a reasoned or constructed truth. It is revelation. Like a wave emerging from the water, what we call the present moment—stars, birds, people, trees, anger, and ideas—arise from the ocean of Undifferentiated Awareness. Practically speaking, the entire cosmos is revealed within the sphere of selfless awareness. This ceaseless revelation is Basic Sanity.

Basic Sanity is the luminous quality of Undifferentiated Awareness that reflects whatever arises without distortion. The body is immune to insanity because it is inextricably connected to the present moment. In the words of Immanuel Kant, the body does not err—not because it always judges correctly, but because *it does not judge at all*. The judging mind can drift off, but the body is rooted in reality. Basic Sanity is indestructible sanity. It is unstained by fear, expectation, or the dualistic perspective of the thinking mind. It is non-stick awareness.

When the mind is tethered to the present moment, we are sane. When we are sane, we are at peace. There is clarity. The light of sanity dispels the darkness of confusion. There is confidence. Anxiety dissipates because there is nothing to prove and nothing to defend. Truth establishes and defends itself.

Incarnation

Novalis said, "The seat of the soul is where the inner world and the outer world meet." *The seat of the soul* is our Incarnation. It is the individuated state of mind and body. In our Incarnation, what is formless becomes physical and what is timeless becomes *timeful*. Taking refuge in our Incarnation means that our words, actions, and presence are inspired by Truth.

---

[5] Genesis 1:3

Incarnation is a state of embodiment where Truth is conveyed, along the lines of reason and action, from the source of intuition to the realm of responsibility. It is the pressing out of Truth into the realm of time and space. Our incarnation is the embodiment of sanity. Fr. Richard Rohr puts it in more religious language when he writes, "The kingdom is wherever God's truth and this world meet and coincide."[6] In other words, the Kingdom of God is established when Truth is brought forth by action—when Truth is incarnate.

These three refuges—Undifferentiated Awareness, Basic Sanity, and Incarnation—are three aspects of one Body. Selfless Awareness and *Truth* are uniquely blended in the song of our Incarnation. This dynamic tri-dimensional body is our True Self. Since it is our True Self, it is always accessible. The openness, clarity, and presence of our True Nature is always there, regardless of how stressed out, angry, or afraid we may be. The only journey we have to make is from the head to the heart. When we take a deep breath and relax, we let go of the false-self and take refuge in the body.

Refuge is not an event but an ongoing process. The practices that follow cultivate our ability to let go of the false-self and reconnect with the body. They are means of taking refuge.

Next, we will turn our attention toward the practice of study.

---

[6] Richard Rohr and Joseph Martos, *Great Themes of Scripture: New Testament*, St. Anthony Messenger Press (1988), pg. 12

7 THE SPACE BETWEEN FUNDAMENTALISM AND ATHEISM

"If you desire wisdom greater than your own, you can find it inside of you. What this suggests is that the interface between God and man is at least in part the interface between our unconscious and our conscious. To put it plainly, our unconscious is God. God within us...If the reader is horrified by the idea that our unconscious is God, he or she should recall that the idea is hardly a heretical concept, being in essence the same as the Christian concept of the Holy Ghost or the Holy Spirit which resides in us all." ~ M. Scott Peck, M.D.[1]

The spiritual path is a return journey. We are walking backwards down the path that gives rise to suffering. Since suffering is a byproduct of disembodiment, spiritual practice works to resurrect the body. When the unconscious wisdom of the body floods the conscious mind, the individuated nature of our True Life is restored. As it stands now, the mind and body are divided against one another. Therefore, we need an interface that enables the two parties to be reconciled. Mythology is that interface.

The word "myth" is often misunderstood. It is either

---

[1] M. Scott Peck, The Road Less Travelled, Simon & Schuster (1978), pg. 281

mistaken as fact or discounted as fiction. Non-believers see mythology as fantasy, antiquated pseudo-science, or an out-right lie. Believers agree with non-believers 99% of the time, the notable exception being the myths to which they subscribe. Their scriptures are exempt from the harsh scrutiny they apply to other sacred texts. As a result, they believe their holy books are infallible. Both camps miss the point. [2]

Myth is a vital part of the spiritual path. It speaks of love, longing, justice, fulfillment, beauty, and transcendence. Mythology transcends historical facts to tell the inner story. It uses the interfacial language of metaphor, ritual, dreams, poetry, art, and parable to tell that story. Mythology opens us up and enables us to study ourselves. For that reason it is an indispensable spiritual tool. But before we pick up that instrument, we need to explore the nature of sacred literature. By necessity this includes a discussion about the dangers associated with religion.

Fundamentalism

In its purest form, religion is perhaps the most powerful vehicle of individuation ever developed by mankind. When

---

[2] When the literalist method is assumed to be the only legitimate method of interpretation, we are forced either to suspend common-sense in order to read scripture or abandon scripture altogether. However, another dimension of scripture opens up when common sense intervenes and suggests that these "paranormal claims" are neither "paranormal" nor "truth claims" but literary devices or symbols meant to communicate a deeper meaning. Fundamentalists protest that symbolic readings attempt to rationalize the text. I agree, to the extent that a symbolic reading utilizes reason to move beyond the absurdities imposed by literalism. This isn't a cheapening of the text but the only possible way to defend the integrity of the text in the face of common sense. For example, reading the virgin birth as a symbol accepts the story as it is—that is as an obvious symbol because in the real world human beings are not parthenogenetic organisms. Reading the symbol is mythologizing, which is why I have chosen to refer to scripture as myth.

religion takes the human condition as its subject and all of its symbols, rituals, and practices work together to improve the individual's quality of life, it is perhaps the most fundamental human undertaking. However, for all of religion's strengths, it has many drawbacks as well. When it gets wrapped up in unearthly concerns that cannot be verified by reason or direct experience, religion becomes a sedative that deadens us to the pain and dissatisfaction of this life by distracting us with the promise of the next. In a word, when religious symbols fail to point past themselves, religion denigrates into fundamentalism.

Religious fundamentalism is responsible for some of the most egregious acts this planet has ever witnessed: war, genocide, terrorism, ecological devastation, and civil rights abuses. Furthermore, religious fundamentalism works on a deeper level to immunize man against the experience of transcendence. When properly employed, myth is an instrument of self-discovery. It points at our life and when we follow its lead, we are brought back to our experience, back to the body. Fundamentalists study books rather than using books to study themselves. They mistake myth as fact and read it like history. This inoculates religion. It says that the transcendent realm is off limits to everyone except the historical embodiment of transcendence that sits on the altar of their tradition. When transcendence is interpreted as a historical event, the possibility of transformation is read out of the myth.

At its core, religion is a path of transformation, so the experience of transcendence is its lifeblood. The possibility of transcendence indicated by the text is the element of scripture that makes it sacred. When this element is taken out of the myth, our sacred texts aren't worth the paper they are written on. When scripture is interpreted literally, the words blot out the substance of the text, *which is within us*, not the book. This leaves the reader identified with the book, instead of the indwelling root of the text. Sadly, this misidentification often leads to the dehumanization of those who do not subscribe to the same book.

Unfortunately, literalism is concerned with events that are limited to a particular time in history and are therefore outside of the realm of personal experience. Therefore, the fundamentalist is an individual who subscribes to a belief system that does not belong to them. They rely upon a book or the experience of another person who relies, interestingly enough, on a book or the experience of someone else. This line of co-dependency stretches back to the source of the tradition, the owner of the original transcendent experience. This is a denial of personal responsibility which leads to idol worship and spiritual laziness.

Literalism is just another word for idolatry. The fundamentalist stands back at a safe distance in envy of a man or woman for having embodied the fullness of their person, but they fail to love and worship that same Power within themselves. "In relation to Christ," writes Kierkegaard, "the wish to admire, or (what comes to the same thing) to worship in admiration, is a falsehood, a fraud, a sin." It turns Jesus into an idol, or as Kierkegaard put it, he obtains admirers rather than followers.[3] Admirers lose themselves in their admiration and as a result fail to make the journey.

Religious fundamentalism offers relief, not transformation. But before it can relieve, it must burden the believer with sin. Once they are saddled with the heavy weight of sin, the preacher

---

[3] Soren Kierkegaard, *Training in Christianity* (Vintage Books 2004), pg. 220

uses the palliative effects of belief to relieve them of their burden. This is the sort of fleeting relief you get by removing ankle weights after wearing them for hours. Since this relief is temporary, the preacher has to perform his trick over and over again. Every Sunday, he has to burden and relieve, which leads to the religious equivalent of a pain-killer addiction.

This spiritual sleight-of-hand fails to bring about real change. The underlying causes of suffering go untreated. After a while the pain and pressure become unbearable. Fundamentalism then directs the believer's attention toward the future, to the next life. It tells them the ultimate release they crave can only be found in the afterlife. So they look forward to the end. In some cases, "the end" refers not just to the end of this life, but to the end of days. This apocalyptic mutation is fundamentalism on steroids. Dooms-dayers romanticize the end of this world and all of its suffering, and in the most extreme cases they take steps to hurry the process along (Branch Davidians or ISIS).

This concludes the section on religious fundamentalism. We will now turn our attention toward its counterpart.

Atheism

Just as all religious people cannot be lumped into the previous section, the following section does not apply to all atheists. The group to which this section refers is a reaction to—and therefore an extension of—religious fundamentalism. We might call them "New Atheists," which is a popular moniker amongst many modern atheists.

New Atheism is the strange bedfellow of religious fundamentalism. The fundamentalist and the New Atheist don't agree on much but they do agree on one crucial point: religious literature should be interpreted literally. They both suffer from the idea that religion is to be treated as a set of truth-claims. Joseph Campbell spoke to this point when he said, "Half the people in the world think that the metaphors of their religious traditions, for example, are facts. And the other half contends that they are not facts at all. As a result we have people who consider themselves believers because they accept metaphors as facts, and we have others who classify themselves as atheists because they think religious metaphors are lies."

The supernatural claims of fundamentalists often wander into the realm of science. And when their claims enter the domain of science, they should face the same intense scrutiny that scientific claims must endure. Most of their claims do not hold water when subjected to critical analysis. But instead of taking the debunked claims of religious literalists as a poor reading of scripture, the New Atheist accepts the basic assumption of fundamentalism. They fervently reject the paranormal conclusions but accept the irrational method of interpretation that generated those claims. They accept the means but reject the end. This turns religion into a straw-man stuffed with wacky paranormal propositions. The New Atheist then demonstrates their intellectual superiority by knocking this straw man over. They set their considerable minds to the task of proving that hobbits don't exist and that Narnia isn't real.

Their efforts may effectively dispel popular superstition, but they overlook the ultimate concern of true religion. Having knocked over the fundamentalist's straw man, they reach the unfortunate conclusion that religion is nothing more than the lingering worldview of ancient man. They conclude that fundamentalism encompasses the circumference of religious thought, and in doing so, throw the baby out with the bath water. This fuels the notion that there is an inherent conflict between science and religion. This is unfortunate. "I don't see any conflict between religion and science," writes Campbell. The real conflict, according to Campbell, is not between science and religion. It is between "the science of 2000 B.C. and 2000 A.D."[4]

Conversion and the Risk of Bypassing

Fundamentalism and New Atheism represent the two poles of thought that dominate much of the religious discourse in the modern West. But many people fall through the cracks of this fatuous debate. The reductionist approach of New Atheism leaves them wanting. They yearn for something more and this craving is not satisfied by a purely rational approach to life. However, they are not buying what the religious fundamentalists are selling either. Modern man is incapable of accepting the claims of fundamentalism. Not only is he intolerant of religious superstition, but he has grown weary of sermons that promote antiquated values. Modern man is looking for something that speaks to his heart without insulting his sensibilities.

Modern man is in search of the space between fundamentalism and atheism. Unable to satisfy this craving at home, Westerners look abroad. But the importation of an exotic religion is not without its dangers. Perhaps the greatest risk with imported religion is spiritual bypassing.

Spiritual bypassing is an attempt to detour the uncomfortable stages of the journey. It can manifest in many ways. For the purposes of this discussion, we are concerned with

---

[4] Joseph Campbell, *The Hero's Journey: Joseph Campbell on His Life and Work*, New World Library (2003) pg. 43

a particular form of bypassing closely linked to religious conversion—though certainly not all conversions are an example of bypassing. It is also important to note that bypassing is a risk inherent in the act conversion. The convert is susceptible to bypassing not because the tradition to which they are converting encourages it, but because the convert carries the risk with them. Often, they are looking for a shortcut, not transformation.

Typically, those interested in adopting a new religion are dissatisfied with or even resentful toward their old tradition. Many come from fundamentalism so their feelings of animosity are understandable. But learning to work with fear, anger, and resentment *is* part of the spiritual path. Transformation is necessarily uncomfortable at times and the spiritual path *always* turns into that discomfort. There are no shortcuts on the spiritual path.

Spiritual bypassing is a sophisticated defense mechanism that attempts to circumvent the uncomfortable stages of the journey. Conversion is bypassing when the convert clings to and identifies with beliefs that do not resonate with them on a personal level *in order to*—consciously or subconsciously—go around the fear and anger associated with their native religion. This is bypassing because the adopted tradition is manipulated to avoid preexisting resentment and contempt. The great spiritual traditions of the world work through our suffering and negativity, not around it. Therefore, it is safe to say that if we are in a roundabout, it is one of our own making.

Conversion is often an external solution to an internal problem. It frequently locates both the problem and the solution outside of ourselves. The false-self uses conversion to blame the old tradition for our suffering or our inability to overcome suffering, and clings to the new tradition as our solution. It wears the new tradition like a costume, masking our fears and resentments with an unnaturally peaceful persona or exotic new belief system. In many instances, these belief systems do not resonate with us in a deep and meaningful way, as evidenced by their inability to arouse the necessary courage to face our disappointment and anger.

Much like New Atheists, many Western converts cling to the straw man offered up by Christian fundamentalists. Their insanity is used to justify our anger and disdain. Instead of letting go of our preconceived ideas and stepping into the discomfort, we righteously cling to the caricature painted by people who believe the world is 4,500 years old and that evolution is a lie from the devil. This places us on the high road. It gives us an air of superiority, but this superiority is vacuous. I am speaking from experience. I struggled with this for years.

My Experience with Resentment and Bypassing

When my parents divorced, I got angry. I blamed god. I expected him to look after me in exchange for devotion and church attendance. Every Sunday I heard that god watches over his flock. Since I believed and my butt was in the pew, I counted myself as a member of the flock. When my parents separated, I figured god was either a fraud or a figment of my imagination, either way I had no use for him. I drifted toward atheism, though there was little rational about it. I was more of a raging atheist. My atheism was not a principled, intellectual stance; anger fueled my athcism. I was mad at god, and any life based on anger is unsustainable.

Eventually, misery overcame me. I started looking for answers. My path brought me to Buddhist meditation, which as a system of practice has been indispensable, but for all of Buddhism's strengths, its mythos never spoke to my heart. I wanted it to, more than anything, but it never did. Still, I held onto it for years. I didn't want to return to the Christianity of my childhood. For me, reading a book about Christianity was like listening to nails scratched across a chalkboard. It made the hair on my neck stand up. So, I held onto Buddhism for dear life.

On both a practical and philosophical level, Buddhism was nourishing, interesting, enlightening, and challenging. Still, the mythical side never resonated with me. The cosmology, reincarnation, the Jataka Tales, all the tantric deities, and guru worship—it was all so alien to me. It felt like my head and my heart were on separate paths.

I remember the first time I found words that struck a chord with me. I was reading a book by the Dalai Lama when I happened upon the name Thomas Merton. The name "Thomas Merton" sounded more accessible than some of the names that graced the covers of books about Tibetan Buddhism. I was fortunate enough to find one of his books—*No Man Is an Island*—on the bargain shelf at a local bookstore, so I picked it up. I knew nothing about Merton other than the glowing recommendation given by the Dalai Lama. As I thumbed through the pages of this book, I became excited. He gave voice to my experience, but not just any voice. He was using a language that resurrected the winds of inspiration deep in my body. Then, without warning, he dropped the C-word: *Christ!*

That one word brought up a host of uncomfortable feelings. I was perplexed, angry, and curious all at the same time. I immediately thought less of Merton. How could such a brilliant and insightful man be Christian? But he wasn't like any Christian

I had heard before. Rather than putting the book down, I kept reading, and I am glad I did.

Ignorance is a key component of bypassing. I never explored Christianity or Judaism. I was unaware of the contemplative traditions embodied by people like Merton. Thomas Merton recast the Judeo-Christian language in a contemplative light. He gave me the words needed to connect the dispersed dots in my head. The practice of Buddhist meditation opened my heart. Buddhist philosophy opened my mind. The Judeo-Christian mythos connected the two. It established an interface that enabled my heart to speak and be heard. With every word, Merton gripped me and brought me deeper into the mystery of my Being, revealing a depth of Western spirituality of which I was previously unaware.

Spiritual Misappropriation

All the world's great religions have a mythological, philosophical, and practical dimension. The practice traditions of the East are, in my estimation, unparalleled. The spiritual practices of India, Thailand, Tibet, China, and Japan are deeper and more comprehensive than anything I have found in the West—and are, by-and-large, devoid of cultural trappings. The philosophical traditions of the East and West are complementary to each other and I have benefitted immensely from my study of both. However, with few exceptions, the mythological components of Eastern religion are exotic and far removed from the Western psyche. So far removed, in fact, that essential practices like prayer are rendered impracticable.

For prayer to be effective, the myth has to resonate with the practitioner. Eastern mythology does not connect with most Westerners. Amitābha and Shiva, for example, do not tug at our heart strings. I would argue that prayer, within the context of an Eastern mythos, is such a strange and irreconcilable practice that most Westerners opt out of it altogether. Since prayer is the most basic application of mythology, its absence leaves a heart-shaped hole in our spirituality.

I do not think Eastern mythology is inferior to its Western counterpart. First, I am suggesting that converts are looking for relief and often looking outside of themselves, which makes them susceptible to spiritual bypassing. Second, in most cases Eastern mythology does not resonate with the Western psyche. Ideas like reincarnation are alien to most Westerners, rendering practices like the Tibetan meditation "All Beings Are My Mother"[5] inaccessible to them. And third, identifying with a mythos that does not enable us to overcome internal strife and reconnect with our True Life is just as disingenuous as the more obvious forms of religious fundamentalism. It is spiritual misappropriation—the substitution of authentic spiritual practice with cultural paraphernalia.

Undoubtedly, this is an unsettling proposition for many. In fact, I imagine that many will set the book down at this point and never return to it. Be that as it may, there is a level of insincerity at play—bordering on hypocrisy—that cannot go without mention. We are standing on the receiving dock, participating in the very practice of religious trade we abhor when it is being exported to foreign lands. We cringe when

---

[5] Tibetans believe in an endless succession of reincarnations. Therefore, all beings have, at some point, been our mother. The "All Beings Are My Mother" practice plays off of this belief. Using the feelings of warmth we have for our current mother, the meditation cultivates and extends a sense of love and compassion toward all beings. It is an effective practice, so long as the doctrine of reincarnation resonates with the practitioner. Of course, reincarnation does not resonate in a deep and meaningful way with most Westerners.

overzealous Christians pour into impoverished African villages under the auspices of "mission work" all the while looking to covert the locals, but we jump on every trendy ship that pulls into our spiritual harbor. I am not saying the teachers from the East are "overzealous missionaries." I am talking about the conversion process. I am saying conversion is an external solution to an internal problem. I am suggesting there is a difference between internal transformation and external conversion. Even His Holiness the Dalai Lama has said, "We have to remain within our traditional religious beliefs. We should not convert."[6]

Reading Our Native Mythology with a New Pair of Glasses

The benefits of reconciling with our root spiritual tradition is one of the central proposals of this book. That doesn't mean we can't practice Buddhist meditation or read the Upanishads. Nor does it mean we have to join our local church or profess Jesus to be the one and only son of God—or even believe that God exists. I am only saying that most Westerners would find it helpful to return to their Western mythos and search for motifs that resonate with them. When we return to the myths of our origin with our feet planted in contemplative practice, the symbols are recast in the light of our inner life and the myth takes on new meaning. Of course, this return will be difficult.

Many of us are working through deep pain and resentment, which is why beginning with the practice of self-analysis is so

---

[6] H.H. Dalai Lama, "Speech at International Buddhist Sangha Conference in Patna, India" (2013), reported by Rahi Gaikwad in *The Hindu*

important. In addition to self-examination, we will have to question much, if not all, of what we know about Western religion. We will have to put our preconceived ideas aside and enter an *apophatic* spirituality—a path of letting go that opens our mind and gives truth the space it needs to reveal itself. This will be taxing, but the effort will prove rewarding.

Myth is in Our Genes

You might be wondering, "Why can't we have spirituality without mythology? Ancient man used mythology to explain his world. Science does that for modern man, so why do we need mythology?" Without question, many of the stories in the Bible served a pre-scientific purpose, but this is only the surface of the text. The primary function of myth is to move beyond the surface and penetrate our inmost core, laying bare our human nature. When we cling to the pre-scientific meaning, not only do we cling to nonsense, but we ignore and discard the deeper role of myth.

The symbols that populate the world's great mythologies are born out of the body. Mankind cannot part ways with myth. He can distance himself from organized religion, but not spirituality and myth. The only question is: What function will myth serve for modern man? Will the supernatural ideas of pre-scientific man continue to hijack our mythological instinct? Or, will myth serve its intended function as a map for the human journey?

"Throughout the inhabited world, in all times and under every circumstance, myths have flourished," writes Campbell. "And they have been the living inspiration of whatever else may have appeared out of the activities of the human body and mind."[7] Mythology is rooted in our biology. It is a part of our makeup to the extent that *it gives voice to our makeup*. Mythology satisfies the desires of our heart without sacrificing the integrity of our intellect. In this sense, mythology occupies the space between fundamentalism and atheism.

Since spirituality is ultimately concerned with embracing and embodying the human condition, and myth is rooted in our very nature, myth is an integral part of the spiritual path. In fact, the study of myth is a spiritual practice, but like all practices there is an element of *how to*. We have to learn *how to* read the map. This chapter is about *how to* read the inner meaning of myth.

There is always a dimension of inner-space beyond words, definition, and explanation. This is the domain of myth. Mythological symbols mediate the relationship between the unconscious wisdom of the body and the intellect. Myth connects the formless realm of truth and inspiration with our rational mind. Our sacred myths are rooted in the transcendent realm of human experience—those aspects of our humanity that escape plain speech. In fact, there is a basic template common to all mythologies.[8]

There is a basic motif predetermined by our biology, but the symbols that populate that template and the language that brings the motif to life are influenced by culture. Archetypal images such as the Divine, the hero, the shadow, and the child-like symbol of innocence, along with the masculine and feminine principles, are ever-present in the world of mythology. But the

---

[7] Joseph Campbell, *The Hero with a Thousand Faces*, New World Library (2008), pg. 1
[8] See mono-myth theory: Joseph Campbell, *The Hero with a Thousand Faces*, New World Library (2008)

feminine principle, for example, will manifest as Tara in Tibet and the *Virgen de Guadalupe* in Mexico. Furthermore, the bond between these mythic images and our psyche are formed early in life. This is why most Westerners would prefer to rediscover the teachings of Jesus than convert to Hinduism.

As an adult, it takes a long time and a lot of energy to establish the deep mythological connections we intuitively form in childhood. So while the motifs of the world's religions are archetypal and recurring, the specific images used to communicate these transcendent principles are culturally conditioned and deeply engrained at the individual level. We have to recognize and respect the conditioned level of our existence because that is where we are. When we return to our native mythology, we honor this fact.

Just as Vishnu cannot be discarded by Hindus for reasons of convenience, the symbols of our indigenous traditions cannot be pushed aside to bypass suffering, nor can they be replaced by the latest trend in New-Age thought. Remember, spirituality is a return journey. We are untying a knot. Since the knot was tied with an extroverted Christian thread, it can only be untied with an interior system of Judeo-Christian symbols. The path of return might be paved by the same words and images, but it is not the same way of thinking. One takes us out of our Self, leaving us discontented and disembodied. The other brings us back to our Self, facilitating reconciliation and wholeness.

Wrestling with the Sacred

When we in the West misplaced "the Divine," it was not labeled "Atman" or "Buddha-nature." It was called "God." Unfortunately, we do not get to choose what resonates with us. Resonance happens before choice. In fact, resonance is a prerequisite for choice. We often accept or reject something based on the effect it produces. But it is worth mentioning that warm, fuzzy feelings are not the only indicators of resonance. "Man's hostility to God," writes Tillich, "proves indisputably that he belongs to him. Where there is the possibility of hate, there and there alone is the possibility of love."[9]

Mythology is a relationship with our inmost nature. Just as interpersonal relationships include trust, fear, anger, and love, a resonant mythology can drudge up resentment and arouse creativity. It is not necessary that we believe anything, but it is necessary that we wrestle with what comes up. Remember, Jacob was given the name *Israel* only after having wrestled with God.[10] It is our job to take what resonates with us and wrestle with it—whether it is good or bad.

Obviously, there are chunks of the Bible that should be discarded: First Century science, prescribed guidelines for slave owners, proper protocol for menstruating women, and directives to stone homosexuals and adulterers, just to name a few. In addition to these unpalatable verses, there are those that simply don't harmonize with a contemplative point of view. Some verses clearly represent a dualistic world ruled by an anthropomorphic god, which is at odds with modern science. However, much of the Bible steers clear of scientific controversy and is open to contemplative interpretation. Scripture does not put forward a unified perspective. How can one book promote varying—and often conflicting—points of view? Because there is not one author.

The idea that there is a single author and therefore a single

---

[9] Paul Tillich, Systematic Theology Vol 2, Univ. of Chicago Press (1975), pg 45
[10] Genesis 32:22-32

intent is a modern fallacy, as theologian and New Testament scholar Marcus Borg explains: "Prior to the invention of the printing press, virtually nobody had seen the books of the Bible bound together in a single volume. Rather, the Bible was most commonly experienced as a collection of separate manuscripts. Indeed, during antiquity and the Middle Ages, the Bible was most often referred to in the plural as 'scriptures'—that is, as a collection of books. Once the Bible was routinely bound as a single volume, it became easier to think of it as a single book with a single author (namely, God)."[11]

Within scripture there are multiple authors and therefore multiple meanings. "The most we can do," writes Jung, "is dream the myth onwards and give it a modern dress. And whatever explanation or interpretation does to it, we do to our own souls as well, with corresponding results for our own well-being."[12]

Reading the Myth Within

Just as the Constitution is open to continued dialogue with the people it serves, so is myth. Interpretation is our side of the dialogue. We must interpret and reinterpret. Of course, "interpret" does not mean using the text to justify resentment or preconceived ideas. As the above quote from Jung indicates, such laziness only wounds our "soul." When I talk about interpreting, I am talking about tracking the text back to the

---

[11] Marcus Borg, *Reading the Bible Again For the First Time*, Harper Collins (2002), pg. 8
[12] Carl Jung, *The Archetypes and the Collective Unconscious*, Princeton University Press (1990), pg 160 quote continued: "The archetype — let us never forget this — is a psychic organ present in all of us. A bad explanation means a correspondingly bad attitude toward this organ, which may thus be injured. But the ultimate sufferer is the bad interpreter himself."

Ground of Meaning within. The true intent of the text is in our heart, not the book.

Myth is a dialogue between the conscious mind and the body. It is our responsibility to continue the dialogue. The initial remarks uttered millennia ago and recorded in scripture are just that, the initial remarks. They beg our ongoing interpretation, just as they will call for the next generation's interpretation.

Most people do not know they are free to interpret the myth in any way that works for them, so long as it is honest and open to continued revelation. They believe they have to accept the understanding handed down to them. This is not true. There are two hard and fast rules in mythological interpretation: follow the myth within and do not stop going. The myth never reads outward and an absolute "Yes!" or "No!" is a dead end.

Since the author of myth is indwelling, it is a mythological axiom to follow the myth within. How do we do that? Rather than getting tied up in the logical inconsistencies that trickle down from a literal reading of religious metaphors, we allow the words to stew while we listen for the resonant echo of the sacred within our body.

The West has a rich and dynamic tradition of following the myth to its indwelling source. Both Judaism and Catholicism have practices that move the individual beyond the literal meaning of the text to its inborn root. Though these practices are relatively unknown, they are centuries-old traditions. We can still make use of these practices today.

One cannot overemphasize the importance of storytelling in Jewish spirituality. Some of the greatest Rabbis have used storytelling as the primary means of transmitting spiritual truths.

The Baal Shem Tov and Rebbe Nacchman, for example, used their unique storytelling abilities to pull back the veil and expose the Divine. This is a Jewish practice as old as the Torah itself.

Myth points past itself to the Truth within us, which is just as true now as it was when the words were written. "The Written Torah is pregnant with meaning," writes Judaic scholar Lawrence Fine. In Judaism, myth is seen as a story with four interrelated levels that pull us closer to truth: *Peshat*, *Remez*, *Derash*, and *Sod*. The first level is historical, legalistic, and at times quasi-scientific. It represents the relationship between ancient man and the world in which he lived (*Peshat*). Beyond the surface, you will find the text hinting (*Remez*) at a deeper meaning—slipping past the historical narrative, allegorically inviting you into the gaps where moral principles are revealed. The third level is an intertextual cross-examination (*Derash*) that uses recurring symbolism and competing commentaries to move beyond morality into the realm of eternal truth. Finally, the myth brings us into the silence of the body where the indwelling source of truth is discovered (*Sod*).[13]

"The sage who combines knowledge of his teacher's tradition with intellectual acumen and spiritual insight," Fine continues, "is himself able to give birth to what appears to be a 'new' Torah, but which is actually as old as the event on Sinai."[14] This *new* Torah tells the continuing story of God's unfolding into the world of time and space through the life of mankind. To participate in this story we have to stop reading scripture like a newspaper. We have to turn the page because we are the next chapter.

---

[13] These four interrelated levels of myth are, to varying degrees, used in the next chapter to paint a picture of Jesus.

[14] Lawrence Fine, "The Unwritten Torah," *The Inner Journey: Views from the Jewish Tradition*, Morning Light Press (2007), pg. 33

In Catholicism, Lectio Divina—which means "Divine Reading"—is the practice of praying the myth back to our center. There are two forms of Lectio Divina: The scholastic version—which is primarily concerned with intellectual understanding—and the monastic form—which moves toward an experience of the Divine Indwelling. Here, we are focused on the monastic strand of Lectio.

In the monastic lineage, "The external word of God in scripture awakens us to the interior Word of God in our inmost being," writes Fr. Thomas Keating.[15] In the practice of Lectio, a small portion of scripture is read mindfully for three to five minutes. For example, take 1 Kings, chapter 19, verses 11-12.[16] Read each word silently and with intention. Don't think about the meaning; just allow the words to settle on your heart. Perhaps a particular verse or phrase stands out. After a few minutes, allow your attention to rest with those words. Maybe the phrase "sound of sheer silence" jumps off the page. Follow it, mindfully repeating those four words, allowing them to lead you deeper and deeper into your body. A few minutes later, the phrase may be reduced to nothing more than the word "silence." Sit with that one word, until you are brought into the inner meaning of the word, into your inner-room, where you rest in the truth of silence.[17]

Clearly, Lectio places the emphasis within the reader, not the book. It invites us to watch the word as it moves beyond the rationale of our exterior self and reaches deep into the formless depths of our Being where the winds of inspiration stir.

---

[15] Thomas Keating, *The Classical Monastic Practice of Lectio Divina*: www.saintandrew.org/assets/centering_prayer/cp_lectio_FrKeating.pdf
[16] See opening quotation in chapter 11
[17] Thelma Hall, *Too Deep for Words*, Paulist Press (1988)

How Does This Relate?

I learned to read the myth back to my Self in a less formal way. Growing up in the Bible Belt, most of the religion I saw was tangled up in extraterrestrial pursuits and I was not interested. Consequently, I was put off by organized religion in general. So when I came to Buddhism, I was somewhat apprehensive. As a stipulation, I swore off any concerns that did not apply to my daily life. I did not bother myself with heaven, hell, where I came from, or where I was going. If it wasn't concerned with this life—here and now—I wasn't interested.

When reading spiritual literature I always ask myself: "How does this relate to my life?" If it is irrelevant, I discard it. If it is relevant, I practice it. Occasionally discarded material later proves to be relevant, and things initially thought to be important turn out to be irrelevant. But this filter—how does it relate to my life?—catches most of the junk and helps drive the message within.

Reading the myth within is like rock climbing: You are looking for the next edge to grip, the next pocket you can use to pull yourself up. We move from one word to the next, from one book to the next. With every inward turn the richness and depth of our inner life becomes more and more obvious. Eventually we realize the myth is originating within us, as if we were reading a story written by someone closer to our Self than we are. Often, that author writes under the pseudonym of God.

The Theistic Perspective

Within every religious tradition there are two currents. There is the exoteric and the esoteric path. The exoteric is associated with outer forms. It is the most popular trend in religious thought. It is popular because it isn't demanding. The esoteric path or mysticism, as it is often called, is the inner path.

In the West, these two currents give rise to two very different forms of religion. The exoteric path cuts us off from the realm of the Divine. Its dualistic obsession with an external deity takes us out of the body, cutting us off from the immediacy and vitality of our True Life. On the esoteric path God is not a name. It does not refer to the highest or most powerful of all beings. It is a symbol. For example, God as creator refers not to a cosmic watchmaker, but the abyss at the center of our Being from which the light of our life and all of creation pours forth.

When "God" is used as a symbol, it "points past itself," as Joseph Campbell once said, "to a Ground of meaning and being that is one with the consciousness of the beholder." This book walks the esoteric path.

Words like God, Tao, and Brahman are necessitated by a basic theism inherent in human experience. This basic theism is the source of the religious impulse in mankind. When I say there is a basic theism inherent in human experience, I do not mean that the belief in a supernatural God is inherent in man. Instead, I mean there is something beyond our normal, waking consciousness. The "Beyond" calls out to us, inviting us to drop the claustrophobic world of the false-self and return to the vastness of our True Life.

This theistic element is present even in non-theistic traditions like Buddhism. "In satori (enlightenment) there is always what we may call a sense of the Beyond," writes the Zen master Shunryu Suzuki. "The experience is indeed my own," he said, "but I feel it to be rooted elsewhere."[18] The "elsewhere" and the "sense of the Beyond" in which the experience of *satori* is "rooted" may be called the Ground of Being, Brahman, Tao, or Buddha-nature. In the West, it is usually called, "God."

Carl Jung described this sense of the Beyond as "a wider unconscious that is never precisely defined or explained. Nor can one hope to define or explain it." Unfortunately, the word "god" is often used as an explanation. This is the exoteric approach. It describes an extraterrestrial superhuman that, having created the world, is charged with the laborious task of overseeing its day-to-day operations. This god fails to speak to the "sense of the Beyond." In such cases, the word "god" is an idol. The anthropomorphic god represents only its obvious meaning, "the highest of all beings, creator and overlord." And the atheist is right to rail against this god, as is the mystic. The god of fundamentalism is not beyond, but apart from. It is not within, but above. Like all threads in the literal narrative, this god is detached and removed from the immediacy of our lives.

"The being of God is Being-Itself," writes the renowned theologian Paul Tillich. "The being of God cannot be understood as the existence of a being alongside others or above others. If God is *a* being, he is subject to the categories of finitude," Tillich concludes.[19] This is worth repeating: God is not a name for the highest of all beings, but a symbol for Being-Itself. This is God beyond god; Infinite Being beyond name and form. "God" does not exist; it is a symbol for existence itself. Thus, it is the final symbol, as it symbolizes the absolute center that is always everywhere. It is the "great symbol" or *Mahamudra*, as it is referred to in Tibetan Buddhism. This is the

---

[18] Daisetz Teitarō Suzuki, *Zen Buddhism: Selected Writing*, Doubleday (1996), pg. 123

[19] Paul Tillich, *Systematic Theology Vol: 1*, University of Chicago Press (1973), pg. 235

unconditional reality that is the underlying concern of all *true religion* because it is the irreducible state of Being from which we cannot be separated.

Salvation and the True Self

We seek the immediacy and vitality of Being—directly or indirectly—in everything we do, because Being is the source of content and therefore the primary cause of contentment. And we all thirst for contentment. We all want to be happy. We yearn to move beyond our limited self and reconnect with the vastness of our True Life. St. Augustine expressed this sentiment when he wrote those famous words: "You have made us for yourself, O Lord, and our heart is restless until it rests in Thee."[20] We are motivated by the experience of Being because in the final analysis we belong to Being-Itself.

Whereas the word God points to an unconditional reality that is beyond all categories of thought, including potentiality and actuality, our True Self represents the movement from potentiality to actuality. The Self is both the *logos* or structure of our Being, and the Incarnation of that structure.

Self (with a capital S) is a verb, not a noun. At the level of potentiality, the Self may be called *spirit*. Spirit is like a blueprint or a seed planted deep in our body that intuits wholeness, fullness, salvation. It is rooted in our inmost nature but its limbs stretch out toward the light of our daily life. Spirit looks to be born into the world through action. It longs to be actualized. This longing is felt as a nudge from within. This guiding presence is the more traditional connotation of spirit, as heard in the phrase "moved by the spirit." It is the drive toward Self-

---

[20] St. Augustine, *Confessions*, Book I

actualization or the unconscious seeking to become conscious.

At the level of actuality, the Self may be referred to as the *soul*, which is a symbol for the individuated experience of mind and body. "Your soul isn't in your body," says Alan Watts. "Your body is in your soul."[21] It is the existential state of Oneness or atonement (at-one-ment). Neither spirit nor soul represents some otherworldly substance. They represent both the drive toward a unified mind and body and the realization of that movement. The realization of wholeness is called salvation.

The word salvation comes from the Latin word *salvus*, meaning, "wholeness, completion, healing." Salvation has nothing to do with reserving our spot in a postmortem utopia by aligning our theological opinions with the edicts of an ecclesiastical hierarchy, doctrine, or sacred text. Salvation is not a matter of subscription, but consent. It is found in the experience of Being—not being this or that, but Being-Itself. Consequently, a sincere religious attitude is defined not by who or what I am, but *that I am*. Salvation is found in the experience of I am-ness. In the book of Exodus when Moses asked God for his name, no name was given. Instead God replied, "I am that I am."[22]

The word "God" represents the power of "I am-ness," which is the central fact of our lives and the source of all religious concern. Salvation is not about saying, "I believe in Jesus or the Buddha." It is a matter of locating the force of Being within ourselves and participating in that force, just as those two men did.

---

[21] Alan Watts, *What is Zen?*, New World Library (2000), pg. 110
[22] Exodus 3:14

The word religion originally meant "to bind together or unite." In its purest form, religion is a system of practice supplemented by an inner mythos that reunites the mind and body.

Mythology seeks to bridge Heaven and Earth, but this is not an extraterrestrial matter. The reunion of God and man doesn't take place in outer space. It unfolds from within, which is why St. Paul instructs his students to "glorify God in the body."[23] For that reason, the essential concern of religious thought is not the origins of the universe, but the health and maintenance of mankind's inner life. This is the responsibility the fundamentalist rejects and the concern the atheist overlooks.

Conclusion

Spirituality in the West is at a crossroads. For reasons that are obvious and all too common, we have become disillusioned with much of Western religion and crave something new. Of late, Western religion seems to be more concerned with ferrying us off to the hereafter and promoting outdated pseudo-science than it is with the reality of our day-to-day lives. We are looking for a down to earth approach—a practical path that embraces our humanity, rather than trying to transform us into otherworldly creatures.

Westerners are in search of a pragmatic spirituality that enables them to live more meaningful and authentic lives. Consequently, many are attracted to the disciplines of yoga and meditation and drift toward the Buddhism and Hinduism sections at the bookstore. As I have stated, this is not a bad thing—in fact, it is a good thing—but we must be careful not to

---

[23] 1 Corinthians 6:20

over identify with foreign mythologies. The wisdom of the East can be a great aid on our journey, but it is an inner journey and as Westerners, much of our terrain is shaped by the Judeo-Christian mythos. I believe we need to take another look at the Judeo-Christian map, but with fresh eyes. The literalist lens we have learned to hold over scripture does not work. Myth is not a telescope; it is an endoscope that enables us to read the story of humanity written on our heart.

This book is not only an effort to flesh out a functioning mythology for the modern West, but an attempt to infuse this mythology with a practice tradition so we may come to embody the mystery that lives within us. The power of God must *transcend history* while simultaneously being *in history*. We have to live it. It is not enough to wax philosophically about the power of God. It must become incarnate through our actions. The experience of God is rooted elsewhere, but it is also our own.

The fundamental metaphor of Western religion, starting with Abraham and coming all the way to Mecca, is "God Is." One could say that "God" is the central metaphor of Western spirituality. Admittedly, "God" doesn't sound like much of a metaphor. Let's say my friend Terry is swimming, and he is a really fast swimmer, so I say, "Terry swims *like* a fish." This is not a metaphor. It is a simile. The metaphor is "Terry *is* a fish." Since the word "God" represents the great reality that is beyond all categories of thought, the only way to formulate the metaphor is to say, "God," "God is," or "God is God"—the last formulation, more or less being the one used at Sinai, "I am that I am." This metaphor points to the transcendent God. Christianity goes one step further.

Christian mythology brings the experience of I am-ness into the world of time and space. It brings God into history. The birth of God into the world through man is the central motif of Christian spirituality. Having addressed the transcendent God, we will now turn our attention toward the incarnation of God through the central metaphor of Christianity, Jesus *as the* Christ.

8 IS IT NOT WRITTEN IN YOUR BOOK?

> *"Most of the Christians I've met would for all practical purposes believe Jesus is God only, and we are human only. We missed the big point. The point is the integration, both in Jesus and ourselves."* ~ Fr. Richard Rohr [1]

At the heart of every myth is a central figure—a hero that invites us to participate in our journey. Initially, our participation is subliminal and vicarious. We get caught up in *their* trials and tribulations, but eventually realize we are caught up in their journey because their journey is a metaphor for our journey. Their stories are presented to us as *our way, our truth, and our life*.[2] When we realize their path to freedom is our path to freedom, our vicarious identification with their journey dissolves into the immediacy of our own adventure.

The central figure in Western mythology is Jesus *as the* Christ. There is a stark contrast between Jesus *as the* Christ and "Jesus Christ." This chapter is devoted to differentiating between the two. The former invites us to say yes to our journey, while the latter places Jesus on a pedestal.

---

[1] Richard Rohr, Religion & Ethics Weekly, pbs.org/wnet/religionandethics/?p=9902
[2] John 14:6

The Boss's Son

On Sunday mornings Jesus's humanity is mentioned only in passing. Miraculous stories that puff up his divinity bellow forth from nearly every pulpit. Such propaganda removes him from the sphere of human concern. This is the Jesus of fundamentalism or as Alan Watts put it, the "Boss's son."

The supernatural Jesus is above tribulation, unscathed by the day-to-day realities of life. He is God only; not man. Furthermore, he is the only one of his kind and therefore irrelevant to us mere mortals. The Boss's son narrative denies the humanity of Jesus because it leads us to believe that by virtue of his pedigree he is beyond temptation. A savior that is beyond temptation is no savior at all because such a figure is above the human condition and therefore could not be more irrelevant to you and I. "Salvation can be derived only from him who fully participated in man's existential predicament," writes Tillich, "not from a God walking on earth, unequal to us in all respects."[3]

Fundamentalist Jesus came down from heaven just as the cool kid Ren McCormack (played by Kevin Bacon) came from Chicago to Bomont with all his fancy singin' and dancin' in the popular 1984 movie, *Footloose*. Jesus walks onto the scene—and occasionally the scene is water—with his blond hair, shuckin' and jivin', while wielding his real life magic powers: the ability to heal the sick, restore sight to the blind, turn water into wine, and raise the dead (including himself). He can do all of this—and we cannot—because he is the boss's son.

---

[3] Paul Tillich, Systematic Theology Vol 2, Univ. of Chicago Press (1975), pg 146

We Don't Want to be Late for Dinner

I know this image is a ridiculous caricature. But put the sarcasm aside and it does, more or less, capture the popular portrait of Jesus. This image tells us more about ourselves than it does about Jesus. The Jesus that graduated *summa cum laude* from the Hogwarts School of Witchcraft and Wizardry is a product of our fear. We are afraid of the adventure before us.

An adventure is a journey, a perilous undertaking that leads to advent. The word "advent" means "the arrival or presence of an important person." In the Christian calendar, the Advent season is the period leading up to Christmas. Fundamentalism reduces advent to singing carols in front of nativity scenes while anxiously awaiting Jesus's long overdue return. It is true that advent looks to the arrival of an important person, but that person is not Jesus. It is you! It is the arrival of your True Self that advent anticipates. When practiced, advent prepares us for the birth of God into the world through our life.

Jesus's life invites us on an adventure and that adventure is our life. "I'm looking for someone to share in an adventure, and it's very difficult to find anyone," says Gandalf in *The Hobbit*.[4] "I should think so, in these parts. We're plain, quiet folk and have no use for adventures," replies Bilbo Baggins. "Nasty, disturbing, uncomfortable things, they make you late for dinner." Much like Mr. Baggins, we don't want to miss dinner. We are sleep walking and don't want to be disturbed. We don't want to face our fear, anger, and self-clinging. We are afraid of adventure. The Boss's Son narrative is written by this fear, and we defend it with our life because to relinquish it is to accept responsibility for our life. If we give up this image, we will be forced to embark upon our

---

[4] J. R. R. Tolkien, The Hobbit, Ballantine Books (1982)

own adventure and that can be scary, as illustrated by the *actual* life of Jesus.

The Boss's Son narrative is a far cry from the picture St. Paul paints of Jesus:

> *"Who, though he was of the nature of God, did not regard equality with God as something to be held on to, but emptied himself, taking the form of a slave, being born in human likeness. And being found in human form, he humbled himself and became obedient to the point of death—even death on a cross."* [5]

Jesus embodied unity with God, but instead of retiring to his Galilean shire to enjoy this unity by himself, he stepped beyond the limitations of selfishness and self-centeredness and followed his journey even *to the point of death*. No small number of people claim to follow Jesus, but how many realize that the adventure Jesus has outlined is one of complete self-abandon? In his death on the cross, Jesus sacrificed every aspect of his Jesus-ness, so his disciples would worship *the Power that animated his life*, instead of his personality. He renounced himself, so that everyone else could hear the good news:

You are a Child of God and He is Pleased with You.

The good news Jesus brought was that we are *anointed* or "called into being" out of the Being of God. "For you created my inmost being," writes the Psalmist, and "I thank you for the

---

[5] Philippians 2:6

wonder of my being, for the wonders of all your creation."[6] Reverberating in Jesus's mind were the words, "God saw everything that he had made, and indeed, it was very good."[7] We know this not only because his baptism and transfiguration echoed these sentiments, but because his life proclaimed that basic goodness.

Rediscovering Jesus

Like the word "God," the name Jesus, when spoken in a room full of people, has the power to arouse both reverence and resentment, often within the same person. Some are inspired by the mere mention of Jesus, while others feel their skin crawl. His name has been used to raise people from the pit of despair, and taped to the end of evangelical baseball bats and used to beat the sin out of moral degenerates. Bitterness and admiration aside, who was this man from Galilee and how are we to understand his life today?

This chapter does not provide a biographical account of Jesus. It is concerned with the modern day import of his life and message. This message is often lost on modern man because it is obscured by the otherworldly presentation of fundamentalists. The outlook of modern man is shaped by the discoveries of science. The claims of fundamentalism are just as unacceptable to the modern mind as flat earth theory. The idea, for example, that Jesus *literally* ascended to heaven is no longer tolerable. "Ascending at the speed of light, Jesus would still be in the galaxy," says Joseph Campbell. "Astronomy and physics have

---

[6] Psalm 139: 13-14
[7] Genesis 1:31

eliminated that as a literal, physical possibility."[8] So how is the metaphor of Jesus *as the* Christ still relevant in a world that is unable to accept literal interpretations of fantastical events like the virgin birth, miraculous healings, resuscitations of the dead, and heavenly ascensions?

The following study employs the interpretive principles discussed in the previous chapter to answer that question. We are following the metaphor within and using it as a tool to study ourselves. How do we follow the myth within? In framing his study of the prophets, Rabbi Heschel explains that "to comprehend what phenomena are, it is important to suspend judgment and think in detachment." This is the methodology of history and biography. "To comprehend what phenomena mean," writes Heschel, "it is necessary to suspend indifference and be involved."[9] This is the methodology of mysticism.

To follow the myth within we must involve ourselves. The meaning of Jesus's life is revealed to us through our involvement because the meaning of his life and the meaning of our life are the same. Therefore, this chapter aims to *involve the reader in the consciousness* of Jesus.

The Central Metaphor of Christian Spirituality

Jesus as the Christ is the central metaphor in Christian spirituality. It is easy to mistake a metaphor for a fact, if you do not know what a metaphor is or how to read one. Remember, the metaphor is not "Terry swims *like* a fish." The metaphor is "Terry *is* a fish." Therefore, the central metaphor of Christianity is "Jesus *is* the son of God," not "Jesus is *like* the son of God."

---

[8] Joseph Campbell and Bill Moyers, *The Power of Myth*, Anchor Books (1991), pg. 67-68
[9] Abraham Heschel, *The Prophets: An Introduction*, Harper Row (1969), pg. xii-xiii

If the metaphor is confused with a factual statement, it paints a disempowering and, quite frankly, bizarre picture of Jesus. When taken as fact, the metaphor trails off into the Boss's Son narrative. On the other hand, when we enter the metaphor, its indwelling truth is revealed and the life of the body is resurrected.

The sacred myths handed down to us from our ancestors are still loaded with meaning because the meaning is within us. Myths are vessels filled by the sacred contents of their readers. They represent a multidimensional, transgenerational dialogue between humankind and the Beyond. This is particularly true of Judaism, which heavily relies upon myth and storytelling to transmit spiritual truths from one generation to the next.

As discussed in the previous chapter, myth is given and received on various levels in Judaism. It starts on the surface with social customs and historical details, but tracks back from there to the indwelling source of meaning. Since the Gospels are (*diasporic*) Jewish books, they too follow this model. "They are written, to a greater or lesser degree," writes Episcopal Bishop John Spong, "in the *midrashic* style of the Jewish sacred storyteller…" The midrashic style he's referring to is the third level in the previous chapter's cross-section of Jewish mythology called, *derash*. "This style," Spong continues, "is not concerned with historic accuracy. It is concerned with meaning and understanding."[10] Meaning, not historicity or biography, is the focus of the present chapter. We will begin with a comparative analysis of the symbolism in the Old and New Testaments, and then move toward the inner meaning of Jesus's teachings.

---

[10] Bishop John Spong, *Liberating the Gospels: Reading the Bible with Jewish Eyes*, Harper Collins (1997) pg. 36

Jesus is the Agent, Not the Principal

Many of Jesus's teachings are in parable, which means they use allegory and symbolism to express meaning. As a result, it is impossible to understand them without understanding the backdrop upon which they are projected. The Jewish mythos is that backdrop. When the myth is separated from the framework in which it was conceived, the essential meaning of the metaphor is lost. So is Jesus. And so are we! This is the current predicament of Western spirituality.

In popular Christianity, the role of Jesus is misunderstood. As Fr. Richard Rohr said in the chapter's opening quotation, "He is God only, and we are human only." This is the worst kind of dualism, the worst kind of idolatry. There is no integration. It essentially turns Jesus into god the sequel. His exclusive identification with the divine establishes him as the source of power—the principal, not the agent. Many Christians think and proudly proclaim on their bumper stickers that "Jesus Saves!" But Jesus doesn't save. It is the Power of Being that saves. In fact, the name *Yeshua* (Jesus) means, "YHWH (I am-ness) is Salvation."

In the First Century, many believed newborn life came from the seed of the father. The man planted his seed in the womb of the mother where it was incubated for roughly nine months. This was a standard belief among the Jewish people which is why, in the book of Genesis, we read that God was displeased with Onan for spilling his seed on the ground.[11] This idea was common knowledge in Jesus's day, and he recast it as a metaphor for man's relationship to God.

---

[11] Genesis 38:9

The early Christian community came to know God through the words and deeds of their teacher,[12] and Jesus painted a radically different picture of God. He referred to God as Father. Obviously, God is neither male nor female. Jesus associated God with the masculine in a mythological sense, not literally. His figurative identification of "God" with "Abba" or the "Father" has several connotations. First, it implies that God is the source of meaning and vitality. Just as the seed of life—according to first century biology—is planted in the woman by man, God breathes into man the breath of life.[13] He is defining God as the source of life, the Ground of Being.

The metaphor of God as the Father isn't just religious sophistry. When internalized, it has practical effects. It encourages an entirely different relationship with the divine. In addition to the obvious implication that we are children of God (which we will discuss shortly), the association of God with the masculine principle implies that mankind is also his consort.[14] The motif of divine union promotes an attitude of openness and willingness; rather than a posture of willfulness. It suggests that our job is to receive life, not generate it. We are called to empty ourselves and become a womb for the divine life.

Jesus applied this principle not only to his disciples, but to himself as well. He described himself as an agent, not the principal: "Whoever believes in me *believes not in me* but in him who sent me."[15] Jesus knew he was not the source of Power. This is the often overlooked distinction between Jesus and God,

---

[12] John 17:17-19
[13] Genesis 2:7
[14] Isaiah 54:4-5— This is also a prominent motif in Indian and Tibetan Mythology.
[15] John 12:44

a distinction Jesus demonstrated time and time again.[16]

Yeshua

Now that the distinction between God and Jesus is established, we can begin to cultivate our understanding of Jesus the man. If he wasn't the source of Power, then who was he? Let us begin with a simple fact: as pedestrian as it may sound, Jesus was a Jew, not a Christian. How did we lose sight of this obvious fact and thereby the context that comes along with it? The short answer: anti-Semitism.

Anti-Semitism has been a part of Christian history since the early days of the Church. Christian history is laced with anti-Semitism for a number of reasons, two of which I will describe here. First, the Jewish authorities rejected the central metaphor of Christian spirituality, relegating the followers of Jesus to the fringe. As Jesus's teachings spread throughout the Mediterranean and the movement separated from its roots in Jerusalem, animosity grew between Orthodox Jews and the Christian Jews throughout the Gentile world.[17] This tension laid the groundwork for future anti-Semitic sentiments within Christianity.

Second, anti-Semitic propaganda was used to absolve Pontius Pilate of blame for Jesus's crucifixion. The Romans

---

[16] These demonstrations are referred to as miracle stories. The miracle stories are often used to support Jesus's unusual abilities. However, the miracle stories are not historical accounts of a divine sorcerer who wandered through the Judean hillside performing magic tricks. They are signs that point past themselves to the power they represent. That is why the first twelve chapters of the Gospel of John are referred to as the "Book of Signs." Furthermore, these signs are invitations for each and every one of us to participate in that power: "Whoever believes in me will perform the miraculous deeds that I am doing and will perform greater deeds than these, because I am going to my Father."

[17] John 9:22

could not tolerate a religion that blamed the death of its central prophet on the governing authorities of the Roman Empire. So, later Christians shifted responsibility over to the already resented Jewish people.[18] This enabled Christianity to gain a foothold in a Roman-dominated world.

One of the unforeseen consequences of this anti-Semitism was the loss of the Jewish perspective that shaped the life of Jesus. I am not taking a jab at Christianity. Rather, I am suggesting that context and meaning are inseparable and pointing out that the well-documented anti-Semitism of Christian history has ripped them apart. In order to reunite meaning and context, we will scan the Old and New Testaments for recurring symbolic themes and use comparative analysis to connect the dots, thereby extracting the essential meaning of the metaphor from the context in which it was conceived.

Jesus was a religious Jew. "Not only is the Hebrew Bible part of the Christian Bible, but it was *the* sacred scripture for Jesus, and the authors of the New Testament," writes Borg.[19] Jesus did not see himself standing outside of the Jewish tradition, but rooted in it. Often this simple fact is stated without considering its profound implications.

Jesus's family was observant. How do we know? The Gospel of Luke goes to great lengths to present Jesus within the context of the Jewish tradition right from his birth: "They performed everything according to the law of the Lord, before

---

[18] Commonly referred to as "Jewish deicide." This doctrine, based on Matthew 27: 24-25, blamed the Jews for the death of God, a strange grievance giving that most of the people that adhere to this doctrine also believe that Jesus's death was foretold and divinely willed.

[19] Marcus Borg, *Reading the Bible Again For the First Time*, Harper Collins (2002), pg. 185

they returned into Galilee, to their own city, Nazareth."[20] Eight days after his birth he was circumcised.[21] When, according to the laws of Moses the time for purification came, his parents took him to Jerusalem to present him in the Temple.[22] But how do we know his parent's religiosity affected his worldview?

"Every year Jesus's parents went to Jerusalem for the Festival of the Passover," writes Luke. On one of those trips the adolescent Jesus disappeared, only to be found *three days* later at the temple impressing a group of Rabbis with his knowledge of the Torah.[23] Judaism was not something forced upon him by overzealous parents. Jesus took to Torah study and Jewish spirituality with enthusiasm. Luke concludes this chapter on Jesus's life by saying, "Jesus increased in wisdom and in stature, and in favor with God and man."[24] Here the Boss's son narrative is reproached.

Luke's account does not describe a prefigured messiah. He says Jesus "increased in wisdom and in stature, and in favor with God." In other words, Jesus did not come into this world with everything figured out. The Boss's son version of the story has Jesus sitting around for twenty-something years waiting to get on with his foretold destiny; whereas Luke's version of the story has Jesus growing physically, psychologically, and spiritually in the manner prescribed by the Torah and the prophets.

The Prophetic Line of Succession

Jesus was steeped in the teachings of Judaism and he

---

[20] Luke 2:39
[21] Luke 2:21
[22] Luke 6:22
[23] Luke 2:41-52
[24] Luke 2:52

participated in the same rituals and customs as his countrymen. But there are elements of his story that place him in a more exclusive class. Jesus's narrative contains elements that not every Jew could put on their resume. The Synoptic Gospels record an instance where three disciples—Peter, James, and John—accompany Jesus to a mountain top.[25] In a vision, they see him standing next to Moses and Elijah.

Jesus stood in the prophetic line of succession and his ministry cannot be understood outside of this lineage. No two figures are more central to the Jewish worldview than Moses and Elijah, and the gospels go to great lengths to interpret Jesus's life through the lens of these great icons.

Everyone knows the story of Moses. He was born during the Egyptian exile. To avoid infanticide at the hands of Pharaoh, his mother hid him along the Nile where he was found by Pharaoh's daughter. She raised him in Pharaoh's court and gave him the name Moses, which is (originally) an Egyptian name meaning "son of." The bearers of this name are considered sons of god, as in the name "Amen-*mose*," meaning "the son of Amen." Later Moses reconnected with the Israelites who were enslaved in Egypt, and led them out of exile. After forty years of wandering through the desert, Moses brought them to the Promised Land.

Similarly, Jesus found himself in the royal court listed not only as a member of King David's lineage, but also counted as the "*son of (mose)* the King of Kings." Additionally, he fled to Egypt to escape infanticide at the hands of King Herod. Moses wandered in the desert for forty years; Jesus for forty nights. And just as Moses called manna down from heaven to feed the

---

[25] Matthew 17: 1-13

Israelites in the desert, Jesus fed the multitudes in a "deserted place" with five loaves of bread and two fish. Like Moses, Jesus led his people out of slavery, but Jesus's exodus was an inner journey out of the bondage of the false-self into the Promised Land of God-consciousness. There are many more similarities between Jesus and Moses, but the Jesus story draws from other sources of inspiration as well, including the prophet Elijah.

The road to the Promised Land cut through the Red Sea for Moses and Elijah split the Jordan. But Jesus parted the heavens while being baptized in the Jordan, symbolizing the inner or "heavenly" nature of his exodus, as opposed to the worldly exoduses of the past. Just as Elijah triumphed over the priests of Baal, Jesus confronted the idolatry of his day, overturning the money lenders' tables and challenging the priestly class. Much is made of Jesus's ascension to heaven, but he is not the first person to ascend to heaven, nor is he the first promised to return. While Jesus ascended into the clouds, a chariot of fire brought Elijah in a whirlwind to heaven. This isn't the last we hear of Elijah, though. The book of Malachi concludes with the following promise: "I will send you the prophet Elijah before the great and terrible day of the Lord comes."

But I Say Unto You…

As you can see, the Power that animated the prophetic careers of Moses and Elijah was also at work in the life of Jesus. The Gospel writers are using preexisting motifs to convey the meaning of Jesus's life and his ministry, but it would be a mistake to think they are saying Jesus is just repeating the escapades of Moses and Elijah. The Gospels portray him as a step forward.

Jesus is taking the Jewish message to the next level, beyond the teachings of Moses and Elijah. This step forward is demonstrated every time the Gospel writers embellish a preexisting symbol or motif. For example, Moses parted the Red Sea, Elijah the Jordan, but Jesus stood in the Jordan and parted the heavens. This practice of recycling and enhancing the myth is a traditional means of Jewish storytelling.[26] Just as Elijah's fiery ascension was an exaggeration of Moses's vanishing act atop Mount Nebo, Jesus's ascent to the right hand of God is an embellishment that hints at a progression from Elijah to Jesus.

When the Gospel writers embellish the symbol, they are suggesting that Jesus's teachings mark an evolution in the collective psyche of the Jewish people—that his teachings transcend the teachings of the previous prophets. This hint also appears every time the words "you've heard it said…but I say to you" are written:[27]

> *"You have heard it said, 'You shall not kill… But I say to you that everyone who is angry with his brother shall be liable to judgment… You've heard it said, 'You shall not commit adultery.' But I say to you that everyone who looks at a woman lustfully has already committed adultery with her in his heart. You have heard that it was said, 'You shall love your neighbor and hate your enemy.' But I say to you, Love your enemies and pray for those who persecute*

---

[26] see discussion of *midrash* in *Resurrection: Myth or Reality?* by Bishop John Shelby Spong, Harper Collins (1995)

[27] Interestingly enough, every interpretation of Jesus's life is an echo of the phrase "You have heard it said, but I say unto you…" Each generation interprets the hero myth in a way that represents the highest ideals of that generation. Therefore, my interpretation does not seek the historical Jesus, but the meaning of that life for the modern age—or better yet, the essence of what is meaningful to modern man. In Jesus, we see our highest Self.

you, so that you may be sons of your Father who is in heaven… For if you love those who love you, what reward have you? Do not even the Gentiles do the same?"

Jesus represents the next stage in the spiritual evolution of the Jewish people. Jesus is not better than Moses or Elijah. He stands on their shoulders as the transfiguration signifies. Jesus is saying it is not enough to mindlessly follow the rules. "Woe to you, scribes and Pharisees, hypocrites! For you tithe mint, dill, and cumin, but you have neglected the weightier matters of the Torah—justice, mercy, trust. These are the things you should have attended to—without neglecting the others!"[28] In Jesus's teachings the emphasis is on the internal, not the external.[29] He does not push Mosaic law aside as so many suggest. Jesus moves beyond the letter into the spirit, revealing the next stage of the journey.

The New Covenant

Moses came down the mountain with Ten Commandments. Jesus went up the mountain and delivered a sermon with eight blessings that constitute a new vision. He set his sights on a new Kingdom, a new promised land, which means a new exodus.

Jesus led an exodus from the outer world of the false-self to the inmost center of man where we are joined to God through the grace of Being, not by the letter of the law. In this new and everlasting promise we are tied to God by our body and blood, not by mindlessly going through the religious motions. This is

---

[28] Matthew 23:23
[29] Matthew 5:28

the New Covenant and with it comes a new vision. This vision is not political, nor is it otherworldly. As far as Jesus is concerned, the Promised Land is not out there or later on.[30] If heaven isn't a postmortem destination or a political kingdom, what *in the world* is he talking about?

The Lord's Prayer begins with "Our Father, who art in Heaven…" In the book of John, Jesus says, "The Father living in me…"[31] If the Father is both in heaven and within me, then it logically follows that heaven is located in the body, not the stratosphere. The body is the Temple.[32] It is the house of God.

In the Gospels heaven is not a celestial abode. It is our inner life. "The kingdom of God is within you," Jesus says in Luke.[9] The words "kingdom," "heaven," and "within" are interchangeable in Jesus's vocabulary. Therefore, to enter the kingdom of heaven we must part ways with our exterior persona. This is well and good in theory, but in practice parting ways with the false-self is scary and uncomfortable. Being true to your Self can be lonely. He who is true to his Self is an outcast in a society where everyone identifies with their external image.

The Revolutionary

The Fifth Commandment given to Moses at Sinai is, "Honor thy Father and Mother." It is said that upon his return Elijah will "turn the hearts of parents to their children and the hearts of children to their parents."[33] Jesus goes in a different direction. He says, "Do not think that I have come to bring peace to the earth; I have not come to bring peace, but a sword.

---

[30] Luke 17:21
[31] John 14:10
[32] 1 Corinthians 6:19
[33] Malachi 4:6

I came to turn father against son and son against father, mother against daughter and daughter against mother, mother-in-law against daughter-in-law and daughter-in-law against mother-in-law."[34]

Jesus sees our inevitable identity crisis—the struggle against familial, social, and religious conditioning—as a gateway to greater intimacy with God and a deeper understanding of our Self. He is challenging us to *be* more and more our Self, rather than trying to *become* who our parents or society would have us be. One day while speaking to a crowd, someone approached him and said, "Your mother and brothers are standing outside and want to speak to you." Jesus replied, "Who is my mother and who are my brothers?" Pointing to his disciples he said, "Here are my mother and my brothers! For whoever does the will of my Father in heaven is my brother and sister and mother."[35] In other words, spiritual kinship is determined by shared values, not genetics, socioeconomic status, or religious affiliation.

Jesus wasn't an anarchist. He didn't promote disorder. Jesus promoted a new order. He advocated a reorientation of values. Jesus did not care who your parents were or what your profession was. He looked past those social fig leaves and asked, "Who are you? Where are you?"[36]

The desire to find and do the will of God is the desire to realize and embody our True Self. This entails a *sacrificing* of one's exterior self-image. Jesus is inviting his followers into a deeper intimacy with God by offering a way of life that flows

---

[34] Luke 12:51
[35] Matthew 12:46-50
[36] Genesis 3:9

against the prevailing norms. In many ways, he is in lockstep with the prophets before him. But when their teachings were used to prop up the status quo, Jesus parted ways.[37] When the teachings of the prophets were used to validate self-righteousness, Jesus raised the bar. "You have heard that it was said, 'You shall love your neighbor and hate your enemy.' But I say to you, love your enemies and pray for those who persecute you. For, if you love those who love you, what reward do you have? Do not even the tax collectors do the same?"[38]

The tax collector has never been a revered member of society, but in Jesus's day they were especially reviled for their greed and perceived allegiance to Rome. While their Roman allegiances are a subject for another time, their greed—or greed in general—is pertinent to the topic at hand. The pursuit of wealth is the great obsession of every society. Sages from time immemorial have railed against greed, but in this obsession Jesus saw more than a social shortcoming. He saw idolatry.

Jesus saw the almighty dollar as the golden calf of his day. When he says, "You cannot serve both God and money," he means that the spirit of the First Commandant goes beyond the domain of pagan gods and graven images. Money becomes a false god when it becomes our ultimate concern. At that point it becomes our master and as Jesus said, "No one can serve two masters. You will be devoted to one and despise the other." He brought the First Commandment into a universal context. While Jesus was definitely concerned with social justice, his teachings did not stop there. His sweeping interpretation of idolatry has implications that go well beyond the world of materialistic concerns.

---

[37] Jeremiah 7: 21-23
[38] Matthew 5: 43, 44 & 46

"You cannot serve two masters" can also be applied to the false-self. The belief that we are separate from God is a form of idolatry. Separation implies autonomy, which introduces a second master—the false-self. This makes us subservient to the false-self with all of its fears and expectations. We cease to be true to our Self and become worshippers of self-will. So, the false-self is also a false god. In fact, the false-self is the first idol, as all other forms of idolatry stem from its roots.

According to Jesus, we have but one master, our True Self, and being true to our Self is the only thing worthy of our ultimate concern. Being true to our Self means carrying this Self into everything we do. This is not the path of laziness left in the wake of the Boss's Son narrative. Essentially, Jesus is saying we "must be perfect, as our heavenly Father is perfect."[39] How can one achieve such a level of perfection?

The Practitioner

"Do not think that I have come to abolish the law or the prophets," Jesus said. "I have come not to abolish but to fulfill."[40] To fulfill means to "bring to completion or fruition." In other words, Jesus came to embody or actualize the principles of the Torah and the prophets. This requires practice.

Jesus was a student, teacher, preacher, and healer, but first and foremost he was a practitioner. "As the word about him spread abroad, many crowds would gather to hear him and to be cured of their diseases. But he often withdrew to lonely places and prayed."[41] According to the Gospels, Jesus frequently *ventured* into the wilderness to *prepare* within himself a path or

---

[39] Matthew 5:48
[40] Matthew 5:17
[41] Matthew 5:15-16

channel *for the Power of God*.[42] Here we see the relationship between adventure and advent playing out. This is what it means to be a practitioner. This is what it means to walk the spiritual path.

The unity of mind and body we crave can be fulfilled only through a life of practice. The central practice on Jesus's path of self-emptying is prayer. Jesus taught that prayer need not be wordy. "When you are praying," he says, "do not heap up empty phrases as the hypocrites do; for they think that they will be heard because of their many words."[43] Like Elijah before him, Jesus found God in solitude and silence.[44] "Go into your inner-room," he instructed, "close your door and pray to your Father who is in secret, and your Father who sees what is done in secret will reward you."[45]

In Jesus's teachings, prayer is not limited to periods of formal practice. Our prayer life must become a life of prayer. We must learn to "pray without ceasing."[46] Obviously, ceaseless prayer is not rattling on incessantly about our fears and desires. If the Lord's Prayer says anything, it says, "Stop! Stop thinking about life. Stop talking about spirituality. Stop asking for stuff! If you want the Kingdom of God to manifest, consent to the will of God. Forgive others, if you want to be forgiven. Take action." This is what "fulfillment" means. When Jesus says he has come not to abolish the law but to fulfill it, he means that his ministry is about living by spiritual principles. Fulfillment has nothing to do with ancient predictions coming to pass, as many believe.

---

[42] Isaiah 40:3
[43] Matthew 6:7
[44] 1 Kings 19:11-13
[45] Matthew 6:6
[46] 1 Thessalonians 5:17

The Suffering Servant

The "Suffering Servant" found in the prophetic writings of the Second Isaiah is another mythic forerunner massaged into the identity of Jesus by the authors of the Gospels.[47] There we find the purest source of inspiration for the life, practice, and ministry of Jesus: "He poured out his soul to death, and was numbered with the transgressors; yet He Himself bore the sin of many, and interceded for the transgressors."[48]

One could argue—and many fundamentalists do—that Isaiah, in a *Nostradamic* fashion, looked into the future and predicted the career of Jesus. They believe the prophets of old saw Jesus in their crystal ball. Fortune telling is a thread in the "Boss's son" narrative. Prophets are not fortune tellers. Rabbi Heschel says, "The main task of prophetic thinking is to bring the world into divine focus."[49] The word prophet means, "one with divine knowledge." The divine is not out there or in the future. It is right now and deep within you. The prophet is not looking into the future, but deep into the present moment. The prophets see so deeply into the present that they see the seeds of the future. And within the structure of the present moment, Isaiah saw the silhouette of a suffering servant.

Jesus and the Gospel writers are looking to their tradition and trusting in the wisdom of the prophets that came before them. In Judaism, study is a transformative practice. The

---

[47] The writings of the Second Isaiah are found in Isaiah chapters 40-55. Second Isaiah is authored anonymously. He is called Second or Deutero-Isaiah because he is profoundly inspired by the Prophet Isaiah. His most influential works are referred to as the Songs of the Suffering Servant.
[48] Isaiah 53:12
[49] Abraham Heschel, *The Prophets: An Introduction*, Harper Row (1969), pg. 24

practitioner enters the myth and is transported from the surface of the story to the Ground of Meaning. It is safe to assume that someone steeped in the Jewish tradition would not only apply these methods to the study of scripture, but retain them as a way of thinking. For Jesus and the authors of the Gospels this was not an extraneous exercise, but a working part of their mind that enabled them to see their mythology as a gateway to the mystery of their life.

The Suffering Servant of Isaiah is one such gateway. It gives us a messianic silhouette, and Jesus brings this image to life. The brilliance of *Isaiah* is found in its deep insight, not in its supposed clairvoyance. The author realized that God is born into the world through our poverty, our emptiness. He looked within and found truth, freedom, and love *in* selflessness. He didn't look into the future and predict the meteoric rise of Jesus's ministry. But rather than arguing this point further, I will put the question to you: which seems more likely—that a prophet of the 8th Century BCE peered 500 years into the future, predicting the birth and career of a Galilean preacher? Or that a man from a small Judean fishing village, who found himself on a collision course with the religious oligarchy in Jerusalem and the might of the Roman Empire, looked back 500 years into his tradition's arsenal to find strength, hope, and direction?

Jesus was distraught about the path before him. The Gospel writers say he was "overwhelmed," "sorrowful," "deeply grieved," and "troubled."[50] Under the shadow of his impending death Jesus searched for hope. He withdrew and prayed, "Father, if you are willing, remove this cup from me…"[51] He found strength, hope, and meaning in the Jewish tradition to

---

[50] Matthew 26:38, John 13:21
[51] Luke 22:41-44

which he belonged. In the Suffering Servant of Isaiah, Jesus found the courage to go from "take this cup from me" to "I am willing."[52]

Isaiah reached out to the downtrodden to "bring good news to the poor...to bind up the brokenhearted, to proclaim liberty to the captives, and the opening of the prison to those who are bound..."[53] Jesus embodies this tradition, but once again, he takes it a step further. In our suffering we are enslaved and imprisoned, but Jesus taught that we are also the jailers. Since we enslave ourselves through various forms of self-clinging, Jesus taught a path of freedom from self instead of freedom from other.[54]

"My kingdom is not of this world," Jesus declared.[55] He didn't mean his Kingdom is in a galaxy far, far away. He meant his teachings do not conform to the world, as Paul explained: "Do not be conformed to this age, but be transformed by the renewing of your minds."[56] Jesus taught that freedom comes from renewing your mind, not rearranging the world. He taught that freedom from anger is contingent upon forgiveness, not revenge;[57] that peace and contentment are found in faith, not self-propulsion;[58] that humility and self-emptying are the path to true Power, not money and clout. "Sell everything you have and give to the poor," Jesus counsels a young rich man. "Then you will have treasure in heaven."[59]

---

[52] Luke 22:42
[53] Isaiah 61
[54] Matthew 5:24, Matthew 7:5
[55] John 18:36
[56] Romans 12:2
[57] Matthew 5:38-39, 6:12
[58] Matthew 6:10
[59] Mark 10:21

In the Sermon on the Mount, Jesus made holy what was thought to be unholy, our suffering and Isaiah helped pave the way.[60] He brought light where there once were shadows: "Blessed are the poor in spirit, for theirs is the kingdom of heaven... Blessed are the meek, for they will inherit the earth. Blessed are those who hunger and thirst for righteousness, for they will be filled. Blessed are the merciful, for they will receive mercy… Blessed are those who are persecuted for righteousness' sake, for theirs is the kingdom of heaven." But he doesn't stop with beatific principles. He practices these principles. "If any one strikes you on the right cheek, turn to him the other also; if anyone would sue you and take your coat, let him have your cloak as well; if any one forces you to go one mile, go with him two miles."[61] This is not a path of self-clinging or moral sophistry. It is a path of self-emptying. This principle of self-emptying defines the life and teachings of Jesus. He called this principle the Sign of Jonah.

The Sign of Jonah

Jesus was "impatient," as Kahlil Gibran observed, "with those who sought after signs in the sky rather than in their own hearts."[62] To those who asked for a sign for the sake of a sign—that is, those who asked for proof—Jesus gave no sign because it could not be received. They are looking outside of themselves for proof of something taking place within them. So Jesus said, "No sign shall be given except the sign of Jonah."[63]

When asked by God to go to Nineveh and "cry out against their wickedness," Jonah refused. Instead, he hopped aboard a

---

[60] Matthew 5:1-12; Isaiah 61:1-3; Isaiah 61:7-10
[61] Matthew 5:38-40
[62] Kahlil Gibran, *Jesus The Son of Man*, The Floating Press (2012) pg. 176
[63] Matthew 12:39

ship and fled to Tarshish. Soon thereafter, "God hurled a great wind upon the sea, and a mighty storm threatened to destroy the ship." Each of the crew members called out to their god for answers and consolation. Neither came. To figure out who was to blame for the storm, they cast lots. The lot fell to Jonah who was sleeping in the bowel of the ship. When they asked Jonah what needed to be done to calm the storm, he replied, "Pick me up and throw me into the sea; then the sea will quiet down for you; for I know it is because of me that this great storm has come upon you." After some time and with great reluctance the crew threw Jonah overboard, but God provided a large fish that swallowed Jonah. From "the belly of *Sheol*," Jonah cried out a prayer of thanksgiving and the fish "spewed Jonah out upon dry land."

The sign of Jonah is self-sacrifice, self emptying. "We must be willing," says Joseph Campbell, "to let go of the life we planned so as to have the life that is waiting for us." Only by surrendering our false-self do we recover our True Self. Jonah's willingness to give up his life, so others might live is the act of abandon that cast his false-self overboard. Like the Passover motif, death sees his sacrifice and passes over him. Jonah's old self was cast aside by his sacrifice and his True Self was spewed out upon dry land. Then Jonah went onto Nineveh to fulfill his purpose. He abandoned his self-centered plans and discovered the miraculous life awaiting him.

Miracle events are symbols that point past themselves to the power they represent. In the myth of Jonah, the miracle is not the giant fish swallowing Jonah or spitting him out *three days later*. The transformation of the Ninevites—"all of them, from the greatest to the least"—is the miracle.[64] Jonah's teachings awakened the people of Nineveh to the presence of God. This awakening was the event through which God was revealed. Likewise, the miracle was not the crucifixion of Jesus, but the resurrection *three days later*. In this miracle, the truth for which Jesus died was resurrected in the body of his followers.

Christ is Not His Last Name

The early Christian community struggled with the death of their teacher. In the sign of Jonah, they found redemption. They found meaning in the selflessness of Jesus. In the absence of his Jesus-ness they discovered the resurrected Christ.

Like Socrates, Jesus died for truth's sake. Throughout his ministry Jesus taught the high principles of truth, love, and nonviolence. In the crucifixion, he practiced these principles. He thought it better to suffer for doing good than to suffer a crisis of conscience. Jesus could have fled or caused an uprising, instead, he walked the *Via Dolorosa*. Rather than resisting evil, he died for righteousness's sake. He died so others—even those that persecuted him, like St. Paul—might find their True Life.

"I came into the world, to testify to the truth," Jesus tells Pilate. "Everyone who belongs to the truth listens to my voice." Pilate asks, "What is Truth?" St. Paul, in his letter to the Corinthians, answers Pilate, "By the grace of God I am what I am."[65] Or as Moses put it, "I am that I am."[66] When we sacrifice our false-self we become transparent and the light of Truth

---

[64] Barbara Rohde, "The Wife of Jonah," *The Inner Journey: Views from the Jewish Tradition*, Morning Light Press (2007), pg. 67

[65] 1 Corinthians 15:10

[66] Exodus 3:14

shines out from the center of our Being. Eventually the light gets so bright that you can no longer see the person, only the light. Such a person is "a light unto the world" or a Christ.

In his death on the cross, Jesus sacrificed every aspect of his "Jesus-ness," including his physical body, so all that remained was the light. But the light was no longer seen through him. The man was no more. From dust he came and to dust he returned.[67] "He was put to death in the flesh," writes Peter, "but made alive in the spirit."[68] He was resurrected in the body of his followers. It took the disciples a while to realize this but when they did, they proclaimed, "It is not I that lives but Christ within me."[69] They experienced the physical resurrection of Christ within their own body, not the resuscitation of Jesus's body. This is the Easter miracle—the seminal event of Christianity.

The question is not whether Christ was resurrected. The question is whether Christ and Jesus are one and the same. The Galilean man who has been the subject of this chapter was not named Jesus Christ as is too often assumed. There was not a mailbox in Nazareth that read, "Christ, Jesus." His name was Jesus son of Joseph (Yeshua ben Yosef). "Christ" is a title attributed to him by his followers. It comes from the Greek word "*Christós*," which is a transliteration of the Hebrew word "*Mashiach*," meaning "the anointed one." Jesus's followers called him the Messiah, the Son of God. So what does it mean to be a Son of God?

The phrase "Son of" implies spiritual descendance, not biological kinship. "It should be understood," says Alan Watts,

---

[67] Ecclesiastes 3:20
[68] 1 Peter 3:18
[69] Galatians 2:20

"that the expression 'son of' means 'of the nature of,' as when we call someone a son of a bitch." Therefore, a Son of God is a person that embodies the divine nature. Jesus confirms this definition when he says, "Whoever does the will of my Father in heaven is my brother and sister and mother."[70] We were all made in the image and likeness of God.[71] When we consent to that image, we reflect that likeness into the world through our actions and become a Son of God or a Christ.

Jesus was a man, just like you and me. And God lives within us, just as It did Jesus. "The point is the integration, both in Jesus and ourselves," writes Fr. Rohr. Jesus was called the Christ because in him the full potential of the Divine image was revealed. He was so transparent to the light of Being that God was born into this world through his actions. Using the metaphor of Jesus *as the* Christ, the Gospel writers situate the reality of God within the body of man and invite us not to admire Jesus, but to participate in the Power of Being just as Jesus did. Our True Self must be resurrected from the tomb of disembodiment.

The indwelling image of God is not only our True Self, it is the Eternal Self—"the image of the invisible God, the firstborn of all creation."[72] This does not mean we are immortal, but that the divine image is now with you, just as it was with Adam[73] and shall be forever more. Your True Self and Jesus's True Self are the same Self. In fact, speaking to this truth was the righteousness for which Jesus was persecuted: "Before Abraham was, I Am."

---

[70] Matthew 12:46-50
[71] Genesis 1:27
[72] Colossians 1:15
[73] The mythical first man in the book of Genesis

The Father and I Are One

"They took up stones to stone him," John writes in Chapter 10, Verse 31. Jesus responds, "I have shown you many good works from the Father. For which of these are you going to stone me?" They answered, as Caiaphas would soon thereafter, "It is not for a good work that we are going to stone you, but for blasphemy, because you, though only a human being, are making yourself God." You see, moments before Jesus said, "The Father and I are one." Steeped in Jewish mythology, as Jesus was, he turned to his stone toting audience and asked, "Is it not written in your book, 'You are gods'?"[74] If those to whom the word of God came were called 'gods'—and the scripture cannot be in error," he skillfully continued, "can you say that the one whom the Father has sanctified and sent into the world is blaspheming because I said, I am God's Son?" Simply put, if I am in error so is the book you believe to be inerrant. Frustrated by Jesus's sharp-witted response, the mob tried to seize him, but he escaped. Later, in the Sanhedrin trial, Caiaphas tried to pin Jesus down once again: "I put you under oath before the living God, tell us if you are the Messiah, the Son of God." Jesus replied, "You have said so. But I tell you, from now on you will see the Son of Man seated at the right hand of Power and coming on the clouds of heaven."

First he tells Caiaphas, "You have said so. But I tell you…" In other words, what you and I mean by "messiah" are two different things. Jesus then unpacks his messianic vision. He describes "a new heaven and new earth" where "God lives amongst mortals."[75] In his vision, mankind is at the "right hand of God." The phrase "right-hand man" refers to someone who

---
[74] Psalm 82:6
[75] Revelations 21:1-3

does the work of another, usually someone more powerful (principal/ agent). Jesus is saying that mankind is the instrument of God's peace and creativity. And that all the kings, queens, and ecclesiastical hierarchies cannot stop this evolutionary force because it is coming on the clouds of heaven. This is the messianic hope of Jesus.

The messianic hope is realized not by a prefigured savior or by a chosen few, but by the whole of society. "Messianic consciousness is not something that comes in the future; it is our intrinsic nature," writes Rabbi David Cooper. "It is our birthright, available to all of us here and now. Although obscured over the millennia by clouds of ignorance, its light continues to shine in the divine sparks at the core of our being… In our time, the goal of raising holy sparks is nothing less than the attainment of messianic consciousness for all of humankind. In this context, the individual cannot be separated from the integrated whole; the collective enlightenment of humanity is clearly as relevant as any focus on individual attainment."[76]

When the messianic impulse is read through the lens of fundamentalism, it leads to complacency. Instead of saying "Yes!" to our adventure, we sit on our hands waiting on our savior. When the messianic myth is read within, it leads to responsibility. We all bear messianic responsibility.[77] "You are the light of the world," says Jesus. "A city built on a hill cannot be hid. No one after lighting a lamp puts it under the bushel basket, but on the lamp-stand, and it gives light to all in the house. In the same way, let your light shine before others, so that they may see your good works and give glory to your Father

---

[76] Rabbi David Cooper, *God is a Verb*, Riverhead Books (1998), pg. 183
[77] In Buddhism, the Messianic impulse is expressed by Maitreya Buddha

in heaven."[78] This is the meaning of "raising holy sparks."

It is our task to transform the world, not by trying to change the people in it, but by recovering the spark of basic goodness that shines within ourselves and elevating that light to new heights. We must allow the flame of God's Being to consume our whole person.[79] When our life is set ablaze by the fires of basic goodness, others feel that flame burning within themselves. This is how the world is transformed.

Conclusion

Just before his arrest Jesus prayed, "Father, the glory you have given me I have given them, so that they may be one, as we are one."[80] Jesus did not see himself as the Boss's Son. He saw the flame of basic goodness in the heart of all men, from the Psalmist to the tax collector: "He makes his sun rise on the evil and on the good, and sends rain on the just and on the unjust alike."[81] His message was a universal one. He did not see man, woman, black, white, gay, straight, Jew, or Gentile. Jesus wanted to speed up the day when all of God's children would answer the call to participate in the Power of God.

Reverberating in the mind of Jesus were the words, "God saw everything that he made, and indeed, it was very good."[82] This "goodness" is at the core of the gospel message. It is the "good news." At his baptism, when the heavens parted, Jesus heard the voice of God say, "This is my beloved Son with whom I am pleased." At the top of the mountain, during the

---

[78] Matthew 5:14-16
[79] Exodus 3:2
[80] John 17:22-23
[81] Matthew 5:45
[82] Genesis 1:31

transfiguration, Peter, James, and John saw the heavens part and heard a voice say, "This is my beloved Son with whom I am pleased."

When we look deep within ourselves, we see that we are good. "Christian life and growth are founded on faith in our own basic goodness, in the being that God has given us with its transcendent potential," writes Father Thomas Keating. "This gift of being is our True Self."[83] The light of our True Life may be obscured by the clouds, but it still shines. We pass through the clouds in silence. Trusting in silence is faith.

Faith has nothing to do with accepting irrational claims. It has nothing to do with belief. Faith is an action. "Take my yoke upon you, and learn from me," Jesus said. The word "yoke" refers to a piece of wood that joins two draft animals together. It shares a family tree with the word "yoga," which means "to unite." When he says, "take my yoke upon you" he means trust my yoga, my practice, my way of life. In short, you must be willing to do the work. You must practice.

On the mantle of Jesus's baptismal confession was the proclamation of basic goodness, the gift of eternal Being—not immortality but *I am-ness*. When we place him at the center of our baptismal confession, we become idolaters. When we place Jesus on our altar, we end up loving him more than we love what he embodied, which lives in our body. When we love something more than the indwelling presence of God, we break the first commandment.

Jesus walked the path *for* us, but not *in place* of us. He blazed

---

[83] Fr. Thomas Keating, *Open Mind, Open Heart: The Contemplative Dimension of the Gospel,* Continuum (1998), pg. 13

a trail, but it is up to us to walk the path. There is no savior coming. The Power of Being must be *resurrected* in *our body* and no one can do that for us. We have to take up the yoke before us. We have to pick up the tools of self-analysis, study, prayer, and meditation.

9 FAITH WITHOUT PRACTICE IS DEAD

> *"The 'way' of Jesus is a universal way, known even to millions who have never heard of Jesus. The way of Jesus is thus not a set of beliefs about Jesus. That people ever thought it was is strange, when we think about it—as if one entered new life by believing certain things to be true, or as if the only people who can be saved are those who know the word 'Jesus.' Thinking that way virtually amounts to salvation by syllables."* ~ Marcus Borg [1]

> *"Do you see that faith was working together with his works, and by works faith was made perfect?"* ~ James 2:22

Misuse of the word "Christ" is not limited to fundamentalists. While they reserve the title for Jesus alone, new-agers often swing to the opposite extreme. They claim that we are all Buddhas and Christs, which is absurd. This is an example of "salvation by semantics." Calling everyone a Buddha or Christ is like handing out spiritual participation trophies.

---

[1] Marcus Borg, *Reading the Bible Again for the First Time*, Harper (2001), pg. 216

When we say that everyone is a "Christ" or a "Buddha," we bastardize the words. When used in this way, they lose their meaning. It strips them of all their symbolic value and turns them into synonyms for "human" or "person." Such fluff reduces spirituality to a naïve and impractical idealism. It leans so far toward the realm of potentiality that it is devoid of practicality and actualization. If spirituality is to be transformative, it must be born into our daily lives. Practice is our midwife.

We are all children of God to the extent that we share in the reality to which the word "God" points. But the title of Christ has greater significance. Christ symbolizes more than our ontological inheritance. It denotes *physical participation* in that inheritance. Jesus is Christ, but not because he was endowed at birth with a power that is alien to us. He is Christ because his life was organized around that Power. Spiritual practice is the effort of organizing our life around that Power.

Jesus was a practitioner. His outer life was tethered to the indwelling presence of God by spiritual practice. "In the morning, while still very dark, he would get up and go out to deserted places and there he would pray alone. Often he would spend the night praying."[2] This is the path he left in his wake. Jesus did not ask his disciples to sit around worshipping him. He asked them to empty themselves as he did. He taught his followers to put away their former life, and clothe themselves with the new Self, created according to the likeness of God.[3] This is no easy task. It takes work.

---

[2] Mark 1:35 and Luke 6:12
[3] Ephesians 4: 22-24

Faith and Spiritual Practice

"Spirituality" is a vague word. It means a thousand things to a thousand different people. More often than not, "spirit" refers to an incorporeal entity that rents out our body. When I say "spiritual," I mean nothing of the sort. Strictly speaking, "spirit" means "breath" or "life," as in, "God breathed into man the breath of life."[4] Spirit is life or Being-Itself. It is the very essence of who we are, our True Self. So "spiritual" means "of or relating to the Self." Therefore when I talk of spiritual practice, I mean a set of actions that transcend the false-self and reconnect us with the vastness of our True Life.

Spiritual practice demands effort but it is a peculiar form of effort. It isn't about doing and learning, but undoing and unlearning. This is the work of letting go. Spirituality isn't the ol' "pull yourself up by the bootstraps" routine. We cannot pull ourselves up. Life rises of its own accord. It is the nature of life to ascend—potentiality moves toward actualization, and the unconscious seeks to become conscious. The false-self tries to freeze the emerging life of the body. Spiritual practice melts away this resistance, so the life that dwells within may be resurrected. Faith is the element in spiritual practice that generates the needed heat. Without faith, practice is cold and mechanical.

Here, faith has nothing to do with believing. We are not talking about wishful thinking. Faith is an action. The act of faith is composed of three qualities: trust, discipline, and open-mindedness. First and foremost, faith lets go of "our world," accepting the world as-it-is. Second, faith holds us accountable to truth. Finally, faith destroys the false-self's siloed point of

---

[4] Genesis 2:7

view by seeking alternative vantage points. Now we will further explore these three aspects of faith and their relationship to spiritual practice.

Faith as Trust

Chiefly, faith is an act of trust. We are trusting in the unformed, selfless awareness of the body. Faith invites us to let go of our old self and move into the darkness of the body where our life originates. This is the core of the kenotic path laid out by Jesus, which might be called the yoke or yoga of self-emptying. This path encourages us to receive our life from within, instead of forcing our life to fit the mold of an exterior self-image. Spiritual practice does not shape the Self. It clears a path for our inner Self to expand into our daily affairs.

The false-self is constantly recreating the world. It thinks about its own thoughts until a dense cloud is cast over reality, obscuring our vision of the present moment. As a result, we do not see reality but what we think *about* reality. We live in a replica of reality. This knockoff world is constantly falling apart, so it is always under construction, which is tiresome. In faith, we find peace and quiet.

When we take the present moment as our starting place, life is straightforward and easygoing.[5] Truth is self-existing. There is nothing to create or maintain. We accept the situation as it is and work with that. This is grace, and faith alone can enter the experience of grace because faith is silent.

Silence is more than the absence of noise. Silence is nonresistance. It is a trust fall into the body. When the mind

---

[5] Matthew 11:30

consents to the truth of the present moment, sanity is restored. In sanity, there is no friction between the conscious mind and reality. The two are One in the body of unformed awareness, so stress and anxiety fall away. In the experience of faith, we find rest for our tired minds.[6]

Faith as Discipline

Faith not expressed in behavior is wishful thinking. Therefore, discipline is a component of genuine faith. Discipline unites action and intention. Spirituality devoid of discipline is pure sentimentality. It clings so tightly to the realm of inspiration that it fails to connect with the world of responsibility and action. It is detached. Perfectionism, on the other hand, leans so heavily on action that it fails to connect with the ground of inspiration and meaning. It is as dry as dust. Both are dead.

Generally speaking, those interested in spirituality have a propensity to be hard on themselves. They often see the world through a distorted lens of right and wrong and become intolerably judgmental of themselves and others. They are plagued by the demons of perfectionism. These demons assume we are working toward a particular outcome. Perfectionism redirects the flow of our life toward that outcome. It bends and twists our True Self, forcing it to conform to our ideas about spirituality.

Perfectionism looks like spirituality from afar, but it is the same vicious process of becoming repackaged in spiritual garb. Perfectionism might say all the right stuff, have all the answers, or hide behind an unnaturally calm persona, but it is just another ego trip. The goal is still to become someone or something in

---

[6] Matthew 11:29

particular, only now we are trying to become holier than thou.

A good person, on the other hand, is not a faultless person who does everything right and never makes a mistake. A good person is a person *of* goodness because, in success and failure, they negate themselves and point back to the source of goodness. They are transparent people who see their victories as moments of clarity through which the light passed, and their failures as opportunities to become even more transparent.

A good person is good because they focus on the indwelling source of goodness, not because they are a goody two-shoes. They are disciplined by their conscience, which is informed by the ongoing revelation of basic awareness. In them, faith is perfected but they are not perfect. In this sense, "perfected" does not mean finished. Faith is never done. Linear perfection is the invention of perfectionism.

Faith takes the immediacy of who we are as the goal to be realized. It meets us where we are. Faith cultivates those often neglected seeds planted in the manure of our imperfection. It goes into our suffering and admits that we are stressed out, confused, angry, or afraid. But faith is not lazy. It never hides behind blame or empty platitudes like, "It is what it is. Progress not perfection." Faith actively pursues perfection. To make progress we have to aim for perfection. What is spiritual perfection and how does it differ from perfectionism?

Spiritual perfection is about consenting to who we are and who we are is forever expanding into the present moment. Shortcomings are not seen as indictments of our character but as opportunities to grow into the fullness of our person. This is what Rabbi David Cooper calls *the model of perfecting*. "With perfecting as our model, we do not need to look beyond what we have because this idea of continuous *perfecting* is in itself perfect."[7] It isn't about arriving; there is no finish line. When we realize there is no conclusion, the emphasis shifts from outcomes to process. When we are honest, open, and willing, our process or spiritual practice is perfect.

Faith is not an event. It is an ongoing participation in the ceaseless revelation that is our True Life. We come back to our Self—back to the present—over and over again. This is an essential point that should not be overlooked, lest our practice become another technology the false-self uses to beat us into a state of unnatural perfection: spiritual practice is about perfectly being, not being perfect. Perfectionism tries to become a god, whereas faith enables God to become human, which is the central concern of Western spirituality.

Faith is always gentle, but gentleness does not mean a lack of accountability. A gentle approach is not a vacation. You cannot take time off from yourself. You go with yourself in everything you do. Who we are is forever expanding, and discipline is our willingness to go along for the ride, even when the journey takes us into rough terrain.

Gentleness means no judgment or beating ourselves up. Beating ourselves up deviates from the path no less than the shortcoming we are beating up on ourselves about. The judgmental voice in the back of our mind is fear cracking the whip of perfectionism. This isn't discipline. It is abuse.

To be disciplined is "to be a disciple." Spiritual discipline is a fidelity to the unfolding of who we truly are. Discipleship is a manner of living that takes our True Nature as the goal. On a

---

[7] Rabbi David Cooper, *God is a Verb*, Riverhead Books (1998), pg. 78-79

fundamental level, our True Self gives purpose and direction to our life. It is who we are and the meaning of life is to *be* that, not to become something else.

From the point of view of our True Self, "the yoke is easy and the burden is light." Everything falls into place and the restlessness of our heart subsides. But, there are two sides to every story. Spiritual practice establishes conscious contact with a selfless reference point. This shifts the balance of hardship from our True Life over to the false-self because the false-self is incapable of relating to this point of no-thingness. The light of basic awareness illuminates what is real and nothing more. So when the false-self stands in front of this mirror-like awareness, nothing is reflected. Consequently, the false-self dies. This is good and well in theory, but in practice it is more difficult.

It is one thing to talk about growth but quite another to suffer the pains of transformation. The false-self system is deeply engrained in our mind-stream. It is our second nature. The first impulse of our second nature is to run when things get uncomfortable. If we turn away every time discomfort pops up, then our practice will only scratch the surface.

You cannot pray or meditate sporadically and expect meaningful transformation. When Gampopa, the founder of the Kagyu school of Tibetan Buddhism, asked his teacher for the highest, most esoteric teaching, his guru, Milarepa, bent over and showed him his calloused butt. Then Milarepa said, "This is my final teaching, persistence. You have to practice meditation every day." Deep and effective change comes from repetition, which is a byproduct of persistence, and persistence depends upon our ability to delay gratification. Therefore, the mark of a mature practice is the courage to persist in the face of discomfort.

Faith as Open-Mindedness

The false-self is closed-minded. It is a control freak. It wants to know what is coming before it gets here. The false-self is afraid to try a new cuisine. It wants to know whether it likes Indian food before it tastes it. This fear is paralyzing. You cannot know Indian food without eating it. We cannot know what will happen before it happens. Understanding is not a prerequisite for action; action is a prerequisite for understanding. We have to step into the unknown. Faith enables us to act without prior understanding. Only faith is capable of stepping into the unknown.

Open-mindedness is the quality of faith that enables us to move forward when we do not know—which is all the time because the present moment is forever being made anew and that which is new cannot yet be known. Open-mindedness accepts this simple fact. It is the courage to explore unforeseen possibilities. In this sense, open-mindedness does not mean we have to entertain every irrational idea. Open-mindedness is the readiness to give up our solid ground. It is the willingness to change vantage points.

The horizon appears to be the earth's edge when seen from the shore. However, when we change vantage points, we see things differently. When we get in a boat and set sail for the horizon, new land emerges from the Beyond. Open-mindedness moves us toward the edge. It is the element of faith that broadens our horizons.

Faith actively seeks new angles that invite fresh information. Prayer and meditation exercise faith. They move beyond the perspective of the false-self, down into the heart where we discover another vantage point. Prayer and meditation invite us to look at life through the selfless lens of the body. For this reason, they are indispensable components of the path.

Now it is time to turn our attention toward the practices of prayer and meditation.

10 PRAYER AND THE TEMPLE

> *"Skillful religionists know that at different times in our lives, we need different faces of God. On a meditation retreat, it is often good to discard all images of the Divine, even the notion of 'Divine' itself, and approach the ineffability of nonduality. In a hospital, this can be extremely unhelpful; there we may need God as healer, as listener, as rock of strength. And in times of emotional pain, we may need some of each. I love that my religious consciousness allows my heart to pine for the God of my ancestors, and connect with Him (and Her) through ritual and the body." ~ Dr. Jay Michaelson*[1]

We are all called to be children of God, but to answer this call we must be willing.[2] Willingness is the active ingredient in transformation. Therefore, spiritual practice must facilitate the transition from an attitude of willfulness to one of willingness. Martin Luther King referred to the movement from willfulness to willingness as the shift from "take this cup" to

---

[1] Jay Michaelson, *Everything is God: The Radical Path of Nondual Judaism*, Trumpeter (2009), pg. 102
[2] John 1:12, Romans 8:14, Galatians 4:5

"nevertheless."[3] Just before his arrest, Jesus prayed, "Father, if you are willing, take this cup from me; nevertheless, not my will but yours be done."[4] Willfulness and willingness are separated only by a semi-colon, but this is the longest journey Jesus ever made. Prayer was the vehicle.

Jesus was "anguished" about the path before him so he withdrew to the Mount of Olives, knelt down and prayed. His prayer begins in willfulness: "Take this cup from me." Jesus is struggling with his fate, but "in his anguish," Luke writes, "he prayed more earnestly…" Prayer seeks to change our perspective, not our circumstances. This is the first principle of prayer and the difference between willfulness and willingness. In order to change our perspective, we must change our vantage point. So Jesus continued to pray until he passed through the clouds of doubt coalescing in his mind and reconnected with his heart where he found the courage to say, "Not my will but yours be done."

Prayer breaks up the false-self's fear-driven monopoly on our attention and turns our awareness to the God of the body. "Do you not know that your body is a temple of the Holy Spirit which you have from God?" asks St. Paul.[5] In ancient Israel, the temple was the house of God. So when Paul asked this question, he meant, "Do you know that God lives in your body?" Prayer answers in the affirmative.

There is a gulf that separates the unconscious wisdom of the body and the conscious mind. Both prayer and meditation work to bridge this gap, though in slightly different ways.

---

[3] Dr. Martin Luther King Jr, *Thou Dear God: Prayers that Open Hearts and Spirits*, Beacon Press (2012), pg. 43
[4] Luke 22:42
[5] Corinthians 3:16

Meditation relies upon silence or formlessness to transcend the divide, whereas prayer relies upon form and symbolism to establish a relationship with God. Prayer and meditation may appear to be distinct practices, but they are two wings of one bird. Both are essential for our spirituality to fly.

Developing a Personal Relationship with God

It is true that *in the final analysis we* are not, in any meaningful way, separated from God. Right now, however, we do not feel the truth of that. Perhaps we are intellectually sympathetic to the idea of Oneness, but we do not currently live in an individuated state. At the moment, we relate to the Beyond as if it were "other than." So we have to start where we are. Prayer is a practice that enters our perceived state of separation.

The experience of God is rooted in the Beyond, but its branches sprawl out into every infinitesimal detail of our daily life. The many names of God—Father, Mother, Witness, Creator, Healer, and Protector—symbolize the various melodies of the divine. These names invite God into our lives, regardless of circumstance. They arouse the Power of Being—which is to say, "the power to resist nonbeing"[6]—in the midst of depression, loneliness, confusion, anger, stagnation, illness, and fear. In this sense, prayer is a very personal practice.

Prayer implies a personal relationship with God. Ramakrishna, the great Hindu saint, says that relating to God only in terms of formlessness is like playing a monotone on the flute, though it has seven holes.[7] Many modern people struggle with the other six holes. We have a hard time reconciling a personal God with our modern, scientific worldview. We need not worry. The term "personal God" does not describe an all-

---

[6] Paul Tillich, *Systematic Theology Vol: 1*, University of Chicago Press (1953), pg. 250-251
[7] Glyn Richards, *Source Book Modern Hinduism*, Routledge Curzon (2004), pg. 67

powerful being that possesses human attributes. "Ordinary theism has made God a heavenly, completely perfect person," writes Tillich, "who resides above the world and mankind. The protest of atheism against such a highest person is correct."[8]

The expression "personal God" describes *our relationship* to God. It does not mean that God is a person. In prayer, we relate to the Beyond in a personal way or "like a person would." When you return home from work and are greeted by your dog at the door, do you bark at him or speak to him like he is a person? Of course, you don't bark. You talk to him like he is a friend or even your child. This is a symbolic gesture that enables you to express feeling and relate to your dog. You may have a personal relationship with your dog, but that does not make your dog a person. He is a dog which is why he doesn't talk back in personal terms.

A personal relationship with God is similar. We may talk to God like a person but this is for our sake, not because God is actually a person. When we take the gesture literally, prayer becomes selfish. Selfish prayer is haggling. It is a willful attempt—and a strange one at that—to rearrange life to our liking. This is not prayer. It is devoid of faith; it is selfishness and self-centeredness all "churched up." In prayer, we are not sitting on Santa Claus's lap telling him what we want and don't want. For prayer to be pure it has to be symbolic—it has to point past our agenda back to the meaning within us.

The Dynamics of Prayer

Human beings have a built in preference for community. Communication is the most common way we seek to commune.

---

[8] Paul Tillich , *Systematic Theology Vol: 1*, University of Chicago Press (1953), pg. 245

We use our words. The division between "I" and "you" is transformed into "we" through the power of language. This is one of the great qualities of human nature. In prayer we seek to commune with God. Prayer skillfully employs language to reunite us with the life of the body.

Prayer makes use of words, but it is not wordy. "The root of prayer is interior silence," say Thomas Keating.[9] An awareness of God's indwelling presence is the source of all things prayerful. When prayer is guided by the principle of faith, the mind is open. This allows the life of the body to pour into the conscious mind, reestablishing the primacy of basic awareness and transmuting willfulness into willingness.[10]

"Language is originally and essentially nothing but a system of symbols, which denote real occurrences, or their echo in the human soul." This quote from Carl Jung shows us how faith transforms our words into prayer. Selfish prayers fail to commune with the body because they denote only the agenda of the false-self. "I want" prayers revolve around "I." They fail to point past themselves. There is no sense of the Beyond. When prayer is faithful, it points past the 'I' to the 'Thou' of the body.

Words have meaning only when they are connected to real experiences. In short, it is experience that gives meaning to the word. Selfless prayer uses words to connect real occurrences in the body with the conscious mind. The following story illustrates the difference between embodied words and words that fail to connect with the source of meaning:

> One day I was walking my dog in the park. I noticed a young couple playing football. They were taking it really serious. She would run a route and he would throw her

---

[9] Fr. Thomas Keating, *Open Mind, Open Heart: The Contemplative Dimension of the Gospel,* Continuum (1998), pg. 14
[10] Psalm 17:15, Romans: 12:2

the ball. Then they would high-five and huddle up. At first, I judged them. I thought, "How weird. They are taking this soooo seriously!" Then I thought, "They are having so much fun, they do not even notice me. They don't care what I think. They are just enjoying each other's company." For a split second, I saw through what I thought about them to who they were. Suddenly an affectionate feeling arose within me. This was a *real occurrence* in my body. But the false-self grabbed it and turned it into an agenda, which was articulated by the following thought: "Man, I got to get me one of those." The false-self hijacked the affectionate feeling. It found the warm fuzzy feeling desirable, so it became the object of my self-centered agenda: "I need to find a relationship like that, so I too can feel what they feel!" It wanted to own the circumstances that triggered the feeling in me, all the while failing to notice that the feeling was already within me. This failure to notice is the only obstacle to realization.

In the story above, my selfish mind reached out instead of turning within. In doing so, the mind separated itself from that which it sought and became needy. When prayer is linked to inborn principles, instead of external circumstances, it points past itself and there is communion. It acknowledges the inborn experience, which broadens the spectrum of awareness to include the totality of our person.

"Prayer is not thinking. To the thinker God is an object," says Rabbi Heschel. "To the man who prays, he is the subject."[11] Prayer is perfected when that to which we are praying becomes the voice uttering the prayer.[12] For example, when we pray for the willingness to change, we are demonstrating the principle we

---

[11] Abraham Heschel, *The Quest For God,* Crossroad (1993), pg. 12
[12] Romans 8:26

seek. It takes willingness to *sincerely* pray for willingness, even if only a kernel. When we overlook this kernel, we sit there with our hands out waiting for willingness to fall in our lap. On the other hand, if we feel the spark of willingness kindling within, we can fan that flame. "Truly I tell you, if you have faith as small as a mustard seed, nothing is impossible."[13]

Prayer is Mind Training

In the beginning, it might be difficult to approach prayer in this way. So established prayers are helpful at first. We cannot expect our mind—which is deeply engrained in its old ways—to produce selfless prayers. If we are used to praying "I want" prayers or are new to the practice altogether, it is likely that our prayer-life will conform to our mind-stream. Traditional prayers are useful because they tend to embody an attitude of willingness. Established prayers are not original, but sincerity makes prayer effective, not originality. When the words of our prayers are accompanied by the sentiments of our heart, prayer is sincere whether we are the author of the prayer or not.

Prayer instructs the conscious mind in the art of willingness. As the words unfold from within, they strip our conscious mind of willfulness, making us more open and receptive to the will of the heart.[14] This is particularly true of the prayer we will use here, the *Prayer of St. Francis*. Though it is widely attributed to St. Francis of Assisi, the actual author of the prayer is unknown. Most believe it to be Fr. Esther Bouquerel, the founder of the French magazine that first printed the prayer in 1912. Despite the source, it remains a perfect example of prayer guided by the principle of faith:

---

[13] Matthew 17:20
[14] Psalm 119:130

Lord, make me an instrument of Your peace;
Where there is hatred, let me sow love;
Where there is injury, may I pardon;
Where there is discord, help me to bring harmony;
Where there is error, help me find truth;
Where there is doubt, may I bring faith;
Where there is despair, may I offer hope;
Where there is darkness, help me shine light;
And where there is sadness, may I offer joy.
O Divine Master, Grant that I may not so much seek
To be consoled as to console;
To be understood as to understand;
To be loved as to love.
For it is in giving that we receive;
It is in pardoning that we are pardoned;
And it is in dying that we are born to eternal life.

We take this prayer to heart by forming each word silently and clearly in our mind's eye, allowing them to fall like a leaf down into the stillness of the body. Every word of this prayer strips the false-self of its willfulness. "Make me an instrument" means "make me a means or a device." We are saying, "Empty my mind, so I may reflect your peace, the peace of the body." Reconnected with the vitality of the body, we no longer feel lifeless or discontented. As a result, we are not worried about what we can take from the world, but what we can bring into it.

God is the light that shines inside. Fear and expectation cut the false-self off from that light. The selfless mind, on the other hand, is free of fear and expectation, so it is at liberty to reflect that light into the world. When we are met with hatred, we can reflect love. We are able to return forgiveness when we are wronged. Where there is divisiveness and conflict, we offer a spirit of unity. Where there is error, doubt, and despair, we return honesty, confidence, and strength. Faced with darkness we reflect light, and where there is sadness we bring joy. We can do this because we are no longer bound by selfishness, fear, anger, or reactivity.

When we surrender to the indwelling presence of God, we throw off the chains of the false-self. This is what it means to be free. We are at peace. Having discovered this great indwelling wealth, we are no longer needy. Therefore, we can seek to console, understand, and love, rather than to be consoled, understood, and loved. We learn that in giving we receive; that our own wounds are healed when we forgive, and that in dying to our false-self, we are resurrected in our True Life. Each word of this prayer points past itself to the Ground of Meaning it represents. In this way, we are disciplined by the prayer.

Many drawn to silent meditation might be tempted to discard prayer altogether. For some it will take a back seat as it did with me. But we should think twice before we dismiss prayer. Prayer and meditation are complimentary. They work together with study and self-analysis to bridge the gap between our True Life and the life we are living.

We can bookend our meditation with prayer. We can begin our meditation practice with a prayer of aspiration that expresses our longing to return to the body. And we can end our meditation with a prayer of dedication that emphasizes the gifting of our Self to the world.

Centering Prayer

When we are praying, we are listening more than we are talking. As Jesus told Martha, "listening" is the one thing of which there is need.[15] In silence we come to know God.[16] Prayer need not be long-winded or eloquent to be effective. One simple

---

[15] Luke 10:38-42
[16] Psalm 46:10

word, like "silence," when said with sincerity, has more power than the prayers of all the televangelists combined. "Thy will, not mine, be done," is the perfect prayer because when said with sincerity, the mind is completely open to the present moment and willing to work with what comes up. Even "amen," which means "so be it," can serve as a vehicle for faith; just one word can bring us back to the body, back into the house of God.

When we are praying, eloquence is not important; it is sincerity and intention that count. In fact Centering Prayer, one of the most profound methods of Christian prayer, makes use of only a word or two. The inspiration for Centering Prayer is spread throughout the Bible, most notably Matthew 6:6. The actual method, however, comes to us from the thirteenth-century treatise on contemplative prayer entitled, *The Cloud of Unknowing*. In recent years, Centering Prayer has gained attention due to the efforts of Fr. Thomas Keating and his organization, Contemplative Outreach.

***

The instructions for Centering Prayer are simple. Choose a word or two as a symbol of your consent to the divine indwelling. Examples include, "Amen," "peace," "trust," "love," "silence," or "stillness." The sacred word symbolizes our willingness to let go—to trust in the unfolding of our life. The sacred word is not disposable. We should use the same word in every session instead of shopping for a new word each time we pray.

Once a symbol has been selected, we take a seat and get comfortable. Then, silently and clearly introduce the word. Remember, the word symbolizes our intent. It is pointing to our heartfelt desire to let go of the stale and claustrophobic world of the false-self. When we say the word with sincerity, we fall down into the stillness of the body. We do not repeat the word like a mantra. When we notice ourselves drifting off in thought, we gently reintroduce the word, rekindling our intent.

Conclude the period of prayer by abiding in the silence of body for a few minutes. Before getting up say a prayer that dedicates the merits of your practice to the world. You can use a prayer of your own or a traditional prayer like the Prayer of St. Francis. The practice of prayer need not be more complicated than this.

Conclusion

Prayer is not for God. Prayer is for the exiled mind that is praying. It is for the conscious mind that longs to return to the body. "Prayer is religion in act; that is, prayer is real religion," writes William James. "It is prayer that distinguishes the religious phenomenon from such similar or neighboring phenomena as purely moral or aesthetic sentiment. Religion is nothing if it be not the vital act by which the entire mind seeks to save itself by clinging to the principle from which it draws its life. This act is prayer… Wherever this interior prayer is lacking, there is no religion; wherever, on the other hand, this prayer rises and stirs the soul, even in the absence of forms or of doctrines, we have living religion."[17]

All that matters is sincerity. We cannot impress the heart with fancy words. Keep it short and simple. When praying, direct the mind toward "the principle from which it draws its life," the body. Pay attention to the indwelling reality that the words represent, not the words themselves. When the words connect, drop them and rest in the body. This is the yoke of prayer.

Now we will turn our attention toward meditation practice.

---

[17]William James, *The Varieties of Religious Experience*, The New American Library (1964), Lecture XIX: pg 352

11 HOW TO MEDITATE WITH THE BODY

> *"Now there was a great wind, so strong that it was splitting mountains and breaking rocks in pieces before the Lord, but the Lord was not in the wind; and after the wind an earthquake, but the Lord was not in the earthquake; and after the earthquake a fire, but the Lord was not in the fire; and after the fire a sound of sheer silence. When Elijah heard it, he wrapped his face in his mantle and went out and stood at the entrance of the cave."* ~ *1 Kings 19:11-13*

The body isn't insulated or protected. It is naked and vulnerable. It simply reflects what is without judgment or evaluation. The self-conscious mind sees this open-door policy with reality as a weakness. And disembodiment is its defense.

The conceptual mind shields itself from the light of our emerging life by stitching together discontinuous thoughts, feelings, and perceptions. Then it lays this quilted image over the body. Only those elements of our life that fit the preformed image are accepted. The rest is suppressed. As a result, much of who we are is rejected. This is the painfully limited nature of the false-self system.

When Adam and Eve became self-conscious, they sewed fig leaves together and made for themselves coverings to hide their naked bodies.[1] But they are only coverings. Behind all of the masks our heart is still beating. The false-self hears this heartbeat. It is haunted by this sound. The false-self knows it is only a covering held over the body. It knows it's a counterfeit. This knowledge is shame.

Shame is the voice of pervasive suffering that constantly reminds us that we are not good enough: not smart enough, strong enough, pretty enough, or ambitious enough. The basic message of shame is "we are not enough." This message haunts us. Instead of listening to shame, the false-self tries to prove it wrong. It tries to prove that it *is* good enough, but every covering it creates is torn apart, which only intensifies our feelings of inferiority. This turns shame into busyness.

When we separated ourselves from the body, we alienated ourselves from the Ground of Meaning. Disconnected from the body, the mind is detached from the world so it has to create its own world. But it knows its creation is inauthentic. Consequently, co-dependency is an innate characteristic of the false-self system. Deep down the false-self knows it is false, so there is a constant need to convince others that the image we are projecting is real. This incessant search for validation is exhausting. Even when we get the desired pat on the back, the sense of self-worth is fleeting. The approval-seeking never ends. We run around trying to prove our worth to people who never questioned it. All the while, we ignore the inner-voice that constantly calls to question our inauthentic life.

---

[1] Genesis 3:7

Downgrading the Mind

Busyness is the false-self's response to shame and insecurity. If our spiritual practice is to be transformative, then it cannot be characterized by this busyness. We cannot think our way out of disembodiment. This is where many of us throw our hands up in frustration. We get mad because thinking about things is all we know. We feel stuck.

Thinking is all we know because we are identified with the false-self and the false-self is the personification of the thinking mind. The thinking mind is personified—or made to look and feel like a person—through an inbred process of thinking that moves the nucleus of who we are up into the space between our ears.

The false-self system is a closed circuit system. It ignores any information that does not originate within itself. It disregards emotion, intuition, inconvenient truths, and challenging points of view. A closed mind cannot feel, listen, trust, be still, or be silent. or silent. It is so closed off that it only sees itself. This breeds corruption. The mind keeps turning to itself to solve problems that it created. In a disembodied mind, the criminal is in charge of the crime scene. If we hope to escape this cycle, we must find another vantage point.

In the West, meditation is often presented as a cerebral exercise. As modern people we live in our head. So we tend to see meditation as a form of mind control. This is misguided. Meditation has nothing to do with controlling the mind.

In meditation, we are allowing the mind to relax down into the body so it may be disciplined by the heart. Contrary to popular belief, the brain does not have authority over the body.

The body is the ground out of which consciousness sprouts. A sane mind is organized around reality, which is revealed in the awareness of the body.

It is the function of the intellect to receive the structure of reason from reality. "Everything that is to be receptive must and ought to be empty," says Meister Eckhart. Therefore, the intellect, in its natural state, is empty. This is original mind.

We are offspring of the universe, made in the image of God. This image lives in the body as our inmost nature. Meditation restores the mind to its original condition so that it may receive this image. Meditation does not empty the mind of thoughts. It moves beyond the apparent solidity of thoughts, ideas, and concepts to discover the underlying emptiness of the mind.

Contemplation

The practice offered in this chapter comes from the Buddhist tradition.[2] It is called *vipaśyanā*, which means "insight" or "looking within." I chose this practice because it is the most direct approach to the body. I did not choose this practice because the West has nothing to offer. Most people believe that silent meditation is unheard of in Western spirituality. They assume that it is an import from the East. In the West, silent meditation has traditionally been called contemplation. Though absent in most churches and therefore unknown to most laypeople, the practice of contemplation has survived in Western monasteries for centuries.

---

[2] For more on Buddhist spirituality, particularly body-based meditation, please see: Dr. Reginald Ray, *Touching Enlightenment: Finding Realization in the Body*, Sounds True (2008)

"What is contemplation?" asks Alan Watts. "It is what you do in the temple," he answers. Paul teaches that the body is the temple.[3] Therefore, contemplation is that which is done in the body. Contemplative practice brings us into the body. It introduces us to the God of the body.

Contemplation is a practice carved out of the Gospels by the Early Christian communities of the desert.[4] While study and prayer can bring us back to the body, only contemplation can enter our depths and abide there. This is because it relies upon silence and silence is the language of the body. This is the traditional meaning of contemplation, but the word no longer carries this connotation in popular speech. It now means "to think over or ruminate." Today the word meditation is more closely aligned with silent, interior practice. While the words are virtually synonymous in my mind, I will use "meditation" from here on out to avoid confusion.

Meditation and the Truth of Shame

On one hand, meditation is an intentional practice. On the other, it is our natural state. The body is always meditating. The practice instructions bring the mind into the body, where the heart teaches the mind to meditate. The instructions do not teach us anything. They just arrange the meeting. The body does all the teaching.

The body gives of itself in perfect silence. Meditation is the practice of receiving this revelation. "I" is the loudest noise we make. "I" adds to and takes away from the revelation of our life more than any other thought. Therefore, when I speak of silence

---

[3] 1 Corinthians 6:19
[4] see *The Wisdom of the Desert*, Thomas Merton, New Directions Publications (1960)

I am not referring to audible silence, but the absence of "I."

What happens when we drop the false-self filter and enter our experience—even the darkest of experiences, like shame? Shame says, "I am not enough: not smart enough or strong enough." The basic message of shame is that "I" is not enough, which is true! When this message is interpreted by the false-self, it is personalized. As a result, we become defensive and shut down. But if we sit in the silence of the body and listen—without the false-self filter—we will hear the truth of shame.

The word "I" is not big enough to embody the vastness of our True Self. This is the truth of shame. "I" does not begin to touch our depths or channel the vitality of our True Life. In its original form, shame is not a self-denigrating message. It is an invitation to a richer, more fulfilling life.

We feel our heart beating from beyond the veil of the false-self. This challenges our inauthentic life. It invites us to return to the fullness of who we are. It is the still, small voice walking through the garden asking, "Who are you?"[5] To paraphrase Trungpa Rinpoche, when the query "Where are you?" is really heard it is regarded as a statement—not a question—and it becomes the answer to the problem of discontentment.[6] We see that our emptiness—the selflessness of our false-self—is not a source of poverty. In fact, selflessness is the womb out of which our True Self is born. But only silence can penetrate this mystery.

We are a mess and the false-self cannot clean it up. But if we sit back and appreciate the mess, the chaos is revealed to be

---

[5] Genesis 3:9 , 1 Kings 19:11-13
[6] Chogyam Trungpa, "The Bardo of Death," *The Collected Works of Chogyam Trungpa: Volume Six*, Shambhala Publications (2004), pg136

intelligent. We cannot organize chaos. Chaos has its own order. We can only observe the chaos in silence and from this vantage point elegance emerges. In fact, chaos *is* order, just not the preconceived order of the false-self. True order is ordinariness. It is *things-as-they-are*.

Sanity is restored when our point of view reflects *Nowness*. It is not our job to create order or logic, but to receive it from the present moment. Everything is where it is and transformation occurs when we consent to this self-existing order (ordinariness), which is the structure of the eternal now (*Logos*). This is what it means for our will to be aligned with God's will. Meditation practice is both the repeated act of consenting to the will of God and the act of abiding in the present moment.

Placing the Body

In meditation, the body is often overlooked. This is unfortunate because, as the Buddhist sage Naropa once said, "In a skillful posture of the body a vital quality of meditation is to be found."[7] Modern people assume that mindfulness is mental concentration. Mindfulness is not focused attention. "Mind" is a word with many meanings. In this case, mind does not mean brain. Mindfulness is not *brainfulness*.

In the context of mindfulness practice, the word "mind" is derived from the Sanskrit root word *cit* which means "awareness." And fullness obviously means "the state of being filled." So mindfulness is the fullness of awareness or decentralized awareness. The practice or application of the

---

[7] Dakpo Tashi Namgyal, *Mahamudra: The Moonlight—Quintessence of Mind and Meditation*, Wisdom Publications (2006), pg. 148

mindfulness principle defrosts our awareness, enabling it to pour into the *fullness* of our person. Mindfulness could just as well be called *bodyfulness*.[8]

Posture and mindfulness go hand in hand. The Kingdom of God might be within, but we need an awareness of our kingship before we can enter the Kingdom. This awareness is authentic pride, which comes from "facing the reality of one's nature," says Trungpa Rinpoche. "It's not a question of becoming what one would like to be, but rather of bringing one's actual energies to full blossom." Posture triggers this blossoming.

We cannot think our way into right thinking, but we can act our way into right thinking. We can change our attitude and outlook on life by changing our actions and the subtlest form of action is body language.[9] So meditation begins with posture or body language.

In meditation practice, we learn to sit like a king. This is a simple, but profound principle. If we see ourselves as a disgusting piece of crap, we will relate to the world like it is one great big toilet. On the other hand, when we see the world through an awareness of our kingship, it is transformed into a kingdom and the people in it become royalty. "I have not encountered another temple as blissful as my own body," says the great Buddhist yogi Saraha. In *bodyfulness*, there is an awareness of our kingship.

It is through our body language that we inherit the earth. Starting today we arrange ourselves with confidence. This confidence is not faux-confidence. We may have to "fake it till

---

[8] Jeremiah 29:13
[9] Amy Cuddy, "Your Body Language Shapes Who You Are," www.ted.com

we make it," but the confidence itself is not contrived. Confidence is a mark of sanity. Sanity is a point of view seated in reality. Therefore when we are grounded in the present moment, we are confident. Truth speaks for itself, so there is no basis for insecurity or paranoia. Like the branches of a vine, the body stretches out into the present moment through the senses. The body is the Tree of Life's root system. When there is an awareness of the body we are connected to the present moment and there is confidence. We cultivate this confidence by holding our posture in meditation practice.

In meditation, our head is upright and supported by the shoulders. There is a natural curvature of the spine that situates our upper body weight on the hips. Our chest is open, and we are breathing naturally. There is a central axis that stretches from the heavens down to the center of the earth, cutting through our core. In a moment of alignment our body is organized along that axis. There is no tension or resistance. Heaven and earth are joined in our posture.

Meditation is a divinely inspired practice. The instructions are manmade, but the human condition is the source of inspiration. Neither the body nor the mind are contorted into unnatural positions. Our anatomy dictates our posture. It doesn't matter if you sit in a chair or on a cushion. What matters is that the body is resilient but open and relaxed.

Practice Instructions

> *"Be still and know that I am God"* [10]

---

[10] Psalm 46:10

Start by arranging your lower body in a comfortable but firm posture with both knees supported if you are on a cushion. If you are in a chair, place your feet flat on the floor about hip width apart. In either case, roll the hips forward slightly, situating your upper-body weight on the hips—not the lower back. Gently pull the shoulders back to further align the torso, ensuring that the weight of the body is supported by the hips and not resting on the stomach. Form a 90-degree angle with the neck and chin. Place your hands palms down on your thighs or in your lap, whichever is most comfortable for you.

You can close your eyes or leave them open. If you notice tension, take a deep breath and allow the weight of your life to relax into the earth beneath you. Rest with a gentle awareness of the body. Make any necessary corrections to your posture by taking a deep breath and allowing the breath to open the body. Once your posture is open, apply the slightest amount of effort to hold the body in its natural resting place. Feel your body being supported by the ground and release any tension down into that support. Practice in this way for about five minutes.

Once the mind has opened up to the body, bring your awareness to the tip of the nose and allow your mind to mingle with the breath. The breath should be soft and natural. As you breathe in, feel the coolness of the air striking your nostrils. When you breathe out, allow your awareness to fall into the body. Continue to work with the breath in this way for five minutes.

Next, drop the breath and allow your awareness to settle with the presence of the body. Bring your awareness to the crown of the head. Feel your hair on top of your head. Allow your awareness to slowly fall into the center of your skull. Just notice any sensations as they arise. Bring your awareness to the forehead and the temples. If there is tightness or tension, allow the tension to fall away with the out breath. Then bring your awareness to the back of your eyes, like there are another set of eyes looking from behind your eyes. Next, allow your awareness to continue to drop, coming down to your nose, mouth, and jaw. Feel the teeth and tongue. Then, bring your awareness to the base of the skull. Finally, allow your awareness to be with the entire head. Observe the difference between the generic image of the head generated by the thinking mind and the experience as it arises within the sphere of unformed awareness. If you detect any tension, release it with the out-breath.

Then, allow your awareness to pour down into the collarbone, the back, the shoulders, upper arms, on into the elbows and the fingertips. Feel your arms tingling in and out of being. Then, bring your awareness back to the collarbone and relax down into your heart-space. Notice the heart beat and the space between heart beats. Watch as the heart arises from nothingness and returns to nothingness. Allow your breathing to become gentler. Take a breath into the heart space and as you exhale, allow your awareness to fall into the upper abdomen and on into the space just behind the bellybutton. Feel your awareness moving from the lower back to the bellybutton. If there is any tightness or tension, take a breath into the abdomen and allow the tension to fall away as you exhale. Now come down into the lowest extremities of the abdomen with the light of awareness touching the anal sphincter, the perineum, and the genitalia. Finally, allow your awareness to be with the whole upper body—from the perineum up to the head. Note the difference between the conceptual image of the upper body held over the light of direct experience and the spontaneous, formless reality that arises within the sphere of naked awareness.

Now, allow your awareness to trickle down through your thighs and hamstrings, on into the knees, working through your calves toward the soles of your feet. Just allow your awareness to rest with the experience of your lower body. Next, observe the difference between the exterior image of the body held over your experience and the immediacy of direct experience arising in the sphere of basic awareness. Rest with your awareness in this space for a few minutes.

Finally, allow your awareness to expand, including all sensations. Notice smells as they arise within the body (light an incense stick before the practice begins). Hear the birds chirp in and out of awareness, but let them be birdless chirps. You do not have to make the chirps birdless. They are already birdless chirps; just let them be as they are. The thinking mind imputes the "birdness" by holding an image of a bird over the chirping. All notions such as sound, chirps, and birds are secondary, conceptual experiences. They are thoughts interpreting and categorizing experience. This is fine. Let it be that way and these thoughts will return to their roots. Just watch as all sensations—including thought—arise and pass away simultaneously.

Thought is a physical sensation. The mind belongs to the body. Thoughts arise within the body of awareness. Just as the heart beats and the lungs breathe, the brain thinks. Like fireflies, they light up the mind and in the same moment they are gone. Thoughts are only problematic when we mistake them for direct experience.

Watch as thoughts arise that say, "Time to get up." Then watch as the next thought says, "No, let's sit longer." Notice how they are both thoughts, sensations in the body, no different than an itch or a stomach growl. Even the thought that says, "They are both thoughts," is another thought. There is no little conductor orchestrating the symphony of experience. "I" is just a thought, a sensation held over our experience. But it is not a big enough container. Experiencing our life from the point of view of "I" is like looking at outer space through a straw. "I" cannot envelope the vastness of our life. So much is left out. This realization will bring you into a deep silence. This is the body of truth. It is your inner room. Rest in this silence.

This silence kills the false-self. Written on the pages of the Talmud is this eerie word of caution: "He and I cannot dwell together in the same space." In the hallowed space of the body the false-self cannot breathe. It dies.

Conclusion

Many modern people ask, "Why doesn't God speak to people like he supposedly did in the day of Moses or Jesus?" Believers ask out of confusion and disappointment, while atheists ask with condescension. But, what if God does speak? Maybe we are asking the wrong question. Perhaps we should ask, "Why don't people listen like they did in the day of Moses or Jesus?"

In point of fact, neither prayer nor meditation establishes contact with God. As the Ground of Being, God is ever-present. The heart is always beating. The heart is always speaking to us, but it is a silent conversation. "God's first language is silence," says Fr. Thomas Keating. The myth of Elijah at Mt. Horeb clearly illustrates this point. Elijah met God, not in the external noise, but in the "sound of sheer silence."[11] God still speaks, but people do not know how to hear the sound of silence.

---

[11] 1 Kings 19:11-13

Many of us believe silence is the proof of absence. We see silence as a question in need of an answer, not as the answer to our question. Mother Teresa once said, "When I pray I say nothing. I just listen." A reporter asked, "What does God say, Mother?" With great depth Mother Teresa responded, "He says nothing. He just listens." Silence is not the proof of absence. It is the womb out of which our True Life is born.[12] That emerging life is characterized by love.

We have yet to talk about love. This is because love is received, not created. It is a gift. When we get out of the way, love rises to the surface. Love is the natural expression of our True Life, unencumbered by the false-self. In other words, love is born out of freedom.

Now we will look at the relationship between freedom and love.

---

[12] Isaiah 30:15

12 THE FREEDOM TO LOVE

> *"By this everyone will know that you are my disciples, if you have love for one another."* ~ John 13:35

The glossy rhetoric that swirls around love attracts many of us to spirituality like moths to a flame. We get all revved up and come in hot. We skip the ground work and, as a result, we burn out. We want to love the poor and destitute, but find it exhausting and overwhelming. We want to love our enemies, but quickly realize this is easier said than done. When the seeds of love are planted in shallow ground, they are scorched when the sun rises. Love bears fruit only when rooted in the deep soil of freedom.[1]

Unconditional love is an expression of unconditional freedom. As long as we are chained to the false-self, we are a slave to its agenda. We do not see our fellow man, but only how they affect us. We see them through the eyes of the false-self, the knowledge of fear and expectation. The ability to love others as our Self is born out of freedom *from* self. It grows out of the freedom *of* God to love our fellow man as they are. So before we can talk about loving others, we have to address bondage or sin.

---
[1] Matthew 13:1-9

Original Sin

The Western conception of sin begins with the fabled events that transpired in the Garden of Eden. The Garden is ground zero for any discussion about sin. As the story goes, God planted the Garden in the east and filled it with "every tree that is pleasant to the sight and good for food."[2] Then he placed man in the Garden and told him "to tend and cultivate it."[3] Recognizing the need for companionship, God later added woman. "And the man and his wife were both naked, and were not ashamed."[4] They were in paradise.

In the Garden, Adam and Eve enjoyed an unquestioned unity with God. But they did not tend to their garden. Obviously, the moral of the story is not that they were bad farmers. We are not talking about a literal garden. The Hebrew word for "mankind" is *adam*, which comes from the word *adamah* meaning, "ground or earth," as in, "God formed *man* from the dust of the *earth*."[5]

The garden is the body. It is the soil out of which our life grows and the plot of land we must cultivate. Adam and Eve neglected this responsibility. This was their great sin.

God told the couple, "You may freely eat of every tree in the garden; but from the tree of the knowledge of good and evil you shall not eat." But the temptation was too great. Adam and Eve wanted more. It was not evil that seduced them. It was the desire for something better. They saw the tree was *pleasing* to the eye and knew it would make them clever, so they ignored God's

---
[2] Genesis 2:9
[3] Genesis 2:15
[4] Genesis 2:25
[5] Genesis 2:7

warning and ate the fruit.[6] With one bite their eyes were opened.

Adam and Eve were not visually impaired before eating the fruit. "Their eyes were opened" is a figure of speech. It means they became self-conscious. They realized that the body was naked and made coverings for themselves.[7] These coverings hid them from the indwelling presence of God.[8] This is sin—alienation, separation, disembodiment. Cut off from the life of the body, they became identified with an external self. And shame came over them.[9]

Like Adam and Eve, we are born into a state of unquestioned unity. And like them, we take it for granted. How could we not? As children innocence is all we know, then life throws us a curve ball. This unity is called into question and we become confused. We anxiously begin thinking about our own thoughts until the illusory world of our imagination appears to be real. Suddenly, it feels like there is a thinker behind those thoughts. Then the cunning and crafty serpent whispers in our ear, "You are that thinker," and we become "like gods."[10] We live in a world of our own making and identify with the creator of that world, the thinking mind.

God told Adam he would die if he ate from the Tree of Knowledge. Despite God's warning, Adam supposedly lived for an astonishing 930 years! The death God warned Adam of was a spiritual death, not a biological one. When we eat of the fruit of knowledge, we migrate up into the lifeless world between our

---

[6] Genesis 3:6
[7] Genesis 3:7
[8] Genesis 3:8
[9] Though not explicitly stated, the idea that the fall resulted in shame is the implication of the pre-fall state of affairs: "And the man and his wife were both naked, and were not ashamed."
[10] Genesis 3:5

ears. We stop living and become identified with what we think about life. This is spiritual death or disembodiment.

Life and death are set before us in every moment. From the Tree of the Knowledge of *Good* and *Evil* falls the fruit of dualistic thinking. This fruit is filled with the seeds of disembodiment, shame, and suffering. Under the Tree of Life we find true freedom, freedom from the false-self. We must choose between the stale and lifeless world of disembodied knowledge and the vitality of the present moment. This is the only real choice we ever make: Are we going to cling to our fears and expectations, the knowledge of good and evil? Or are we going to accept life as-it-is? If we cling to the former, we are bound by the fear-driven agenda of the false-self. If we choose the latter, we are set free. This choice defines our life.

Falling into Freedom

The myth of the Garden is a timeless motif. Its staying power is owed to its deep connection with the human condition. We are all born into perfect unity and we all misplace that unity. This is not a judgment of our moral character. It is just a fact: we all fall from the individuated state. We live east of Eden.[11]

Sin is separation from God. Since God lives within the body, sin is disembodiment. Original sin refers not only to the state of separation, but to mankind's inherited predisposition to mistake words and ideas for the realities they represent. The concept of original sin suggests that disembodiment is foreshadowed by our human nature. In other words, the fall is fate, not punishment.

---

[11] Genesis 3:24 (Adam and Eve went East when they exited the Garden)

On one hand, freedom is an essential quality of our inmost nature. On the other, freedom cannot be compulsory. To actualize freedom we must consent freely. We must come by it honestly, or it isn't freedom. The state of involuntary unity does not stick. We take it for granted *because* it lacks consent. It is potential freedom, not actualized freedom.

Exile is not the punitive will of a cosmic overlord as it is often described. "The fall" is inevitable. We are thinking, imagining creatures. We are bound to taste the fruit of our knowledge—to mistake the images of our imagination for the realities they represent. The unity of mind and body has to be challenged. We have to die a spiritual death to be resurrected.

Just as exile is a possibility within the structure of unity, atonement (at-one-ment) exists as a possibility within the condition of exile. "The power of God," says Tillich, "is that He overcomes estrangement, not that He prevents it."[12] The spiritual path sees our misidentification with the ego as part of our development. Just as it recognizes the fall as a stage of our journey, spirituality sees the opportunity to throw off the false-self and recover our True Nature as a part of our human maturation. We have to be deceived by a forgery before we can develop an appreciation for the genuine article. In short, we all lose ourselves, because in finding our Self we gain a degree of depth and fulfillment that is otherwise unobtainable.

On Earth as it is in Heaven

In truth, the separation between man and God is an illusion. We are not actually separated from God. God is a

---

[12] Paul Tillich, *Love, Power, and Justice: Ontological Analyses and Ethical Applications,* Oxford University Press (1954), pg. *112-113*

symbol for *Being-Itself*, which we participate in through our Being. We could not separate ourselves from the reality of God even if we wanted to. This inability to be estranged from the presence of God is what Matthew Fox calls "Original Blessing," and Original Blessing cannot be trumped, not even by original sin.[13]

Our life is rooted in the presence of God, not sin. God lives in the body as the life of the body. Sin is a figment of our imagination. We only think we are separated from God. "The chief thing that separates us from God," writes Fr. Keating, "is the thought that we are separated from Him. If we get rid of that thought, our troubles will be greatly reduced. We fail to believe that we are always with God and that He is part of every reality. The present moment, every object we see, our inmost nature are all rooted in Him."[14] Every sight, sound, idea, feeling, smell, and sensation arises from the Ground of Being. This may be a nice sentiment, but to realize it we have to let go of the idea that we are a solid, separate self.

"The only true joy on earth," writes Merton, "is to escape from the prison of our own false-self, and enter by love into union with the Life Who dwells and sings within the essence of every creature and in the core of our own souls."[15] If we cling to the false-self with its fear, resentment, ambition, and stress, then we are too bloated to pass through the eye of the needle. With all that baggage we cannot enter the Kingdom of our Being because the gate is too narrow.[16] Only the simplicity of our True Self can fit through the gate because the gate is a cut out of our True Self.

---

[13] Matthew Fox, *Original Blessing : A Primer in Creation Spirituality*, Bear & Co (1996)
[14] Fr. Thomas Keating, *Open Mind, Open Heart: The Contemplative Dimension of the Gospel,* Continuum (1998), pg. 44
[15] Thomas Merton, *New Seeds of Contemplation*, New Directions Book (2007), pg. 25
[16] Matthew 7:14

God's will is often described as if it were a cosmic scavenger hunt: "God wants me to go to college, find a job, get married, have 2.5 kids, attend this church, and buy a boat." We spend our whole life looking for God's will, but never find it. Why? Because we have confused self-will with God's will. Self-will is extraneous, busy, and needy. What is God's will? In reality, God does not have a will for you.

The will of God is the *image of God* in man as his essential nature. "God does not want to be believed in, to be debated and defended by us, but simply to be realized through us," writes Martin Buber.[17] God wants to become you. In short, you are the will of God. The will of God is fulfilled when our inmost Self is brought into the world through our actions. Or, to paraphrase the Lord's Prayer, "The Kingdom comes when God's will is done on earth as it is in heaven."[18]

While God may be present within us as "our inmost nature," this nature remains dormant until we consent. The act of consent is consummated with action. Action is the final stage in the process of *act*ualization, which means, "to embody." In short, God is born on earth through our actions. "Our world" becomes "the Kingdom" when the light of God illuminates every aspect of our life.

The light of awareness must shine out from the center of our Being onto every relationship, every interaction, and through every thought, word, and deed. This is a tall order and we will fall short many times. Our daily practice gives us a foundation. Personal inventory, study, prayer, and meditation make us more transparent, enabling the light of our True Life to shine on all of

---

[17] Martin Buber, *On Judaism, Schocken Books* (1995), *pg. 94*
[18] Matthew 6:10

our affairs. Though a daily practice is indispensable, we cannot stop there. Our spirituality cannot be limited to a list of daily chores. For spiritual practice to be effective, we must bring the principles of personal inventory, prayer, and meditation into our day. Love makes that possible.

The Power of Love

On the spiritual path, we will fall short many times. It is easy to become impatient, frustrated, and overwhelmed. That is why love is so important. Love sees life in everything. It recognizes the life that abides within every creature. This recognition begets respect. Love is patient, kind, and endures all things, as anyone who has attended a wedding knows. Our knowledge, plans, and strategies will reach their wit's end, but love never tires.

One day, while watching my favorite television show, *The Office*, I heard those famous words of St. Paul's yet again[19] but this time with new ears because I was holding my newborn son. As I looked at him and heard, "And now these three remain: faith, hope and love. But the greatest of these is love," I understood. For the first time, I understood.

In that moment, I knew: I knew that I could read every book in the world and make plans from now until the end of time, but my knowledge would be exhausted and my plans would fall short. No strategy and no amount of preparation could ever get me to the finish line. The only thing that remained was love. Only my love for him can bear the hardships and difficulties that our relationship will bring to the surface. Only my love for him can overcome my impatience and arrogance.

---

[19] 1 Corinthians 13:3-13

Only my love for him can guide him without trying to bend him to my will. Only love is humble enough to teach him *how* to think without teaching him *what* to think. For only the eye of love sees him as his own person and only love is selfless enough to grant him the space he needs to grow into that person. Love is the only voice within me honest enough to admit that he does not belong to me.

Truthfully, it is not "my" love and it is not "for him." Love is the defining characteristic of the Kingdom. I do not create love. I receive it. Love is a gift.

"Whoever does not love does not know God, for God is love."[20] And as children of God, we resemble God. Love is our birthmark.[21] When freedom from self is realized the likeness of God is reflected in our actions. The cataracts of fear and expectation are removed and we can see the world as-it-is. When we recover the freedom to see people as they are, we see the life that dwells and sings within them, and love is our natural response.

Throughout the pages of this book I have placed considerable emphasis on man's inner life, not because it's more important than man's outer life, but because it is the spring from which our outer life flows. The indwelling image of God is the fount of love that erupts at our center, breaking through our skin onto the plane of our Incarnation. Such love sees beyond the projected self of others to their inmost depths where their True Self abides. When the eye of God within us makes contact with the eye of God in our fellow man, there is communion, which is the meaning of "Namaste."

---

[20] John 4:8
[21] John 13:35

I cannot teach people how to love. To my knowledge, no one can. Love is wild. It has no manners. It comforts the afflicted, and afflicts the comfortable. Love often defies logic. It would have us embrace our enemies and be uncomfortably honest with our friends. This cannot be taught. Love does not come with a manual. It is the spontaneous expression of our True Nature.

I am hesitant to talk about love, but I'm more reluctant to say nothing. I am afraid that if left unfastened, the truth of love will be reduced to an ambiguous and miasmic sentiment that fails to connect the reality of our True Self to the responsibilities of our daily life. So now we will turn our attention to love, which consists of three qualities that correspond to the three modes of Being discussed in chapter six.[22] Those three facets of love are unconditional love, gratitude, and creative love.

Unconditional Love

As I said before, love is complete freedom—the freedom of God to love friend and foe as our Self. Love is complete and total freedom because it is selfless. Selfless awareness is wide open, *agapic* awareness.[23] This is the all-embracing quality of *Undifferentiated Awareness* that recognizes and embraces everything that is real and true, regardless of whether it is comfortable or not.

Self-centeredness is the worst kind of prison. It keeps us chained and shackled to our fears and illusions, reserved to making decisions that serve our own narrow-minded agenda. Love doesn't see the world or the people in it through the

---

[22] Undifferentiated Awareness, Basic Sanity, and Incarnation
[23] *Agape* is the highest form of love in Greek philosophy.

knowledge of good and bad. Love does not see what we stand to lose or gain. It sees things-as-they-are. And when you see things-as-they-are, you see the spark of divinity that lives within all things.

Gratitude

In the embrace of unconditional love, it feels like we are loved *into* Being. This awareness brings about a phase change. It transmutes the energy of unconditional love into gratitude. Dominion is not control, but responsibility.[24] Gratitude accepts this responsibility. When you are grateful for something, you "tend to it." When God told Adam to tend to the Garden, he meant love it—love the body, your fellow man, and the earth.

Gratitude is an action, not an idea. It is the act of caring for that which we are grateful. Gratitude doesn't hang out in the oceanic presence of unconditional love. It reaches out to the world *from* the deep space of love. It invests, not only in the maintenance of our Self, but through likeness recognizes and welcomes the True Self in others. Likeness is a quality of *Basic Sanity*. It looks beyond race, religion, gender, sexual orientation and social status to find its kind in others. In this way likeness gives rise to kindness, which is the foundation of relationship. Having established relationship, love goes through yet another conversion.

Creative Love

At this stage, gratitude and kindness give way to the creative power of love. The principle of *Eros* or erotic love isn't limited to "sexual desire." It refers to the creativity of love.

---

[24] Genesis 1:26

Therefore, sexual union is both an example of Eros and a most useful symbol for its creative nature. We are born *out of* love and therefore born *to* love. Love is the Alpha and Omega.

Eros is the desire to *make* love. It is the creative force that seeks to express love through relationship, art, poetry, music, prayers of devotion, and songs of worshipful silence. Eros articulates love. In fact, creative love is art—it is the aspect of love that lends shape to the unformed inspiration of our inner life. Eros is love *Incarnate*.

While creative love is the principle that underlies the great works of art, it is not limited to painting, music, or theater any more than it is to the bedroom. In fact, creative love is most active in our daily life. It is the aspect of love that expands the field of practice. It brings our spiritual practice out of our home and into our day.

Love in Daily Life

The Upanishads say, "And then He realized that he was this creation, as it had poured forth from Himself. In this way He became this creation. Therefore, he who realizes this becomes, in this creation, a creator." To become a creator is to bring the divine image to fruition. Having discovered an untapped inner wealth, we are no longer dominated by our poverty mentality. We are full. We seek to give back, to create.

Eros transforms our life into an art form. It is the art of living. When we consent to the power of love, it shapes our life in the same way Michelangelo chiseled his sculpture of David from raw stone. This happens in relationship. We cannot wall ourselves off from the world and call it spirituality. Without relationship our practice is incomplete. Commitment connects the responsibilities and obligations of our daily life to the indwelling reality of our True Self.

Committed relationships are difficult because they demand that we give of our Self. This is hard because the false-self is selfish. It wants to avoid discomfort and clings to immediate gratification. Creative love matures us by reminding us that we cannot hope to grow into our True Self without something demanding our false-self in return.

The resurrection of our True Life is proportionate to the death of our inauthentic life. The false-self is incapable of accepting this truth. It is bound to itself. Love is free to accept this maxim. This is the power of love to endure all things: marriage, divorce, success, failure, friendship, rivalries, heartache, and death. The freedom of love enables us to adapt to life's changing circumstances. From the point of view of creative love, there are no problems, only opportunities. If the problem can be solved it is not a problem, just something for you to work with; if it can't be solved, it is not a problem, just something to accept and move on. Creative love sees everything as workable.

Eros recognizes disappointment as part of our path. It doesn't see tribulation as something to be avoided. The Dalai Lama once said that we cannot view a beggar as an obstacle, if we hope to grow in generosity. This axiom can be applied to all other virtues as well. Patience is an indispensable spiritual principle, but when given the opportunity to grow in patience, many of us reject it. We rail against the person trying our nerves. We label those who try our patience as "assholes," but without an obstruction or an "adversary" there is no growth.[25] Creative

---

[25] The Hebrew name Ha-Satan translates as "the adversary." The adversary was not originally a villain. Satan, as clearly illustrated in the book of Job, was more like the

love knows that we cannot grow in patience without an asshole in our lives and binds our actions to this principle.

Without struggle there is no growth which is why Shantideva writes, "All enemies are helpers in my *spiritual* work and therefore they should be a joy to me."[26] Where there is an enemy, a shortcoming, or an obstacle, creative love sees a gateway. When we are angry, afraid, jealous, depressed, or obsessed, love knows there is an underdeveloped aspect of our Self struggling to be born into the world. Love seeks to cultivate it. It loves our devils into the present moment; it does not reject them. We may be intellectually sympathetic to this idea, but only the power of love recognizes this on a practical level.

What we call spiritual principles live within us as potentialities embedded within the structure of Being, but just as the capacity to walk is a potentiality that has to be exercised by toddlers, these potentialities have to be actualized through the struggle of daily life. In this way, God is born into the world.

Spirituality is about accepting our obstacles as the path, not avoiding them. Only love is capable of seeing the relationships and tasks that present us with difficulty as the plots of land that we must cultivate. In short, what we call obstacles, love calls the path, and all paths intersect.

Conclusion

If we look closely, we will see an intricate web of

DA in the court of God. He would go out and identify shortcomings and prosecute those defects of character, in order to bring people closer to God. See the book of *Job* 1: 1-12

[26] Shantideva, *The Bodhisattva's Guide to the Way of Life,* Shambala (2006), pg. 92
*The original text uses the word "*Bodhisattva*" (awakened being) not "*spiritual.*"

interdependence emerging. It may appear that we are attracted to this person or that job for one reason or the other, but if we look closer—beyond the veil of the false-self—we will see that the power of love has brought us into this relationship. "Driven by the forces of love, the fragments of the world seek each other so that the world may come to being," writes Teilhard de Chardin, the brilliant Catholic theologian.[27] It is as if the universe is working as a midwife, assisting in the birth of our Self. But love is never a one-sided situation. The forces of love are at work in the other person as well. The universe is using us to assist in their birth. There is something deep in the other that yearns to be realized, and it has identified a relationship with us as part of its path. We are there to aid in their birth, just as they are there to aid in ours.

While love may bring us together, it does not chain us to one another. It binds us to the truth in our hearts. So in love, there is solitude. "For the pillars of the temple stand apart," writes Kahlil Gibran, "and the oak tree and the cypress grow not in each other's shadow."[28] Selfish love—which is no love at all—sees the other as an object to be exploited or a hostage to be taken; authentic love recognizes the symbiotic structure of the relationship. A healthy relationship moves back and forth between solitude and communion. It sees both interdependence and independence.

The longer we stick with this process, the more obvious it becomes that we are not in control. We are just along for the ride. There are forces beyond the jurisdiction of our conscious mind that arise out of the darkness of the body and organize our life. It is our job to be disciplined by these forces. So in the

---

[27] Teilhard de Chardin, *On Love & Happiness*, Harper & Row (1984), pg. 43
[28] Kahlil Gibran, *The Prophet*, Chapter 3

words of the great Muslim poet Rumi, "Let yourself be silently drawn by the strange pull of what you really love. It will not lead you astray." This strange gravitational force pulls toward a center that is both within us and outside of us. This force is the will of God. In the final analysis we realize that our life is not our own. We live in the Mind of God.

13 THE MIND OF GOD

> *"A human being is a part of the whole, called by us 'Universe,' a part limited in time and space. He experiences himself, his thoughts and feelings as something separate from the rest—a kind of optical delusion of his consciousness. The striving to free oneself from this delusion is the one issue of true religion."* ~ *Albert Einstein*

Love awakens us to a strange and wondrous world, a world characterized by Oneness. This is not a manufactured unity. It is not a fragmented world assembled with parts that are themselves incomplete. It is a Universe—a world so complete that within each part the whole is found. This universe is contained within the present moment, the Mind of God.

We envision time in a linear way. We assume that life started in the past, moves through the present, and proceeds forth into the future. This linear representation is a self-centered version of time. In truth, the past is an echo of Nowness. When the original sound was uttered it was Now, and when the future arrives, it will be Now. Furthermore, the past and the future exist as nothing more than memories and expectations arising within the present moment. Now is the absolute, eternal center that is always everywhere—past, present, and future.

We participate in Nowness through the basic awareness of the body. There is a kaleidoscope of sensory information received through the sense gates. At the conceptual level, this information is divided up into various groupings—sight, sound, smell, taste, touch, emotion, and thought—but these are just classifications. From an experiential point of view sound, sight, touch, smell, taste, emotion, and thought aren't different forms of awareness. They are waves of information arising out of and crashing back into the ocean of basic awareness. They are lines drawn in the sky of Nowness.

Things and Thinks

Unfortunately, we do not live from the point of Nowness. We have eaten the fruit of knowledge and as a result are lost in the field of duality. We do not see the world *as it is;* instead we see our version of the world—what we "think" about "things."

Wisdom is immediate or unmediated while knowledge is second-hand. Knowledge is our analysis—a measurement—of life, not Life-itself. Alan Watts cleverly illustrated this point using an analogy: To measure a curve, you install points. You fix upon this crooked line various points and measure the distance between them. Well, life is a curve. Life is fluid and to measure it we install fixed reference points. These reference points are "things."

Things are thoughts. They are practically the same word, as Watts pointed out when he said, "a *thing* is a *think*."[1] A thing is an idea, a name, a point used to measure our experience, a curve.

As mentioned in previous chapters, "thinks" are not

---

[1] Alan Watts, *Eastern Wisdom, Modern Life: Collected Talks 1960–1980*, New World Library (2006), pg. 77

problematic. They are useful constructs that enable us to measure our world and communicate with one another. Problems arise when we mistake the map for the territory. It is our attachment to "things" that proves to be problematic.

The false-self is a concept that is defined by its relationship to other things. It is literally attached to things. Since things are thinks, a "thing dependency" is an addiction to thought. We think about our thoughts until we lose sight of the surface we set out to measure.

Thought is not excluded from the body, but when thought fails to point past itself to the real occurrence it represents, the body is excluded from thought. A disembodied mind is an insane mind. Insanity transforms the present moment into a *thing* that falls under jurisdiction of "I," the original *think*.

The word "I" does not refer to the totality of our person. It refers to a sliver of our person localized in the dome of the skull. "I" is the personification of the conceptual mind. It is the phantom behind every operation of our life: the owner (mine), actor (I did), thinker (I was thinking about), and the one in charge (I decided). It is devoid of all symbolic value and therefore incapable of pointing past itself. "I" references only that which made the reference, thought. So, it creates a self-referencing loop and leaves us stuck in our head.

This self-referencing loop is an obsession and with obsession comes speed. Much like an airplane propeller, the faster our thoughts spin the more solid they appear to be. As the speed increases, the tension collects between our ears. Before long we are two, four, sixteen, thirty-two thoughts removed from the present moment. "I" starts to look more like a solid disk, rather than four or five blades spinning in space. The cloud of thought becomes so thick that we can't tell the difference between reality and fantasy. As a result, we mistake our personal narrative for truth. We replace the immediacy of basic awareness with the fruit of second-hand knowledge.

The Emptiness of Other

Though we passionately believe in the autonomy of self-will, it is an illusion generated by inbred thought. This illusion is like a knot tied in the thread of awareness, which disrupts the flow of *Nowness*. This knot is the root of all suffering, a seed of insanity that has fallen from the Tree of Knowledge. So let's work through its apparent solidity and untie the knot. We will start with an inanimate object, instead of a person. Starting with an inanimate object enables us to gain familiarity with the process of inquiry without getting tripped up by self-clinging. We will start by tearing apart a car in search of its "car-ness."

Here is a car: four doors, four tires, a hood, fenders, a trunk, motor, steering wheel, the whole bit. We all assume this is a car, but "car" is actually just a concept. It is a *thing* that refers not to an object that can be singled out and identified, but to a collection of parts that perform an expected function. At the conventional level this concept is useful, but if we disassemble the car, looking for its "car-ness" or its "I," we will find no such thing because the *thing* we are looking for is actually a *think*.

If I took a ratchet and removed the hood, asking, "Is this the car?" you would respond, "No, it is the hood not the car." So I would proceed to remove the tires, the doors, the fenders, etc. I would remove all the external components and for each part I would ask, "Is this the car?" to which you would respond, "No, it is only a part of the car." Then I would move on to the more essential parts. I would remove the alternator, transmission, battery, and engine, and each time ask, "Is this the car?" and every time you'd respond, "No, it is a part of the car."

Eventually, the space once occupied by the car would be empty. You might say, "The car is not in any one part, but in the sum total of parts." So I would turn to the pile of disheveled parts behind me and ask, "Is this the car?" and you would respond, "The car is not found in any one part or in the basic sum of parts, but in the proper assembly of those parts." In other words, all the parts must not only be present, but arranged in a workable order before they are awarded the designation "car."

When a bunch of car-less parts are arranged in a working order, we call that arrangement a "car." It possesses no sense of self or "car-ness" from its side. We see "car-ness" because we see it from our side. We see the concept "car" or what we think, not reality.

There is nothing wrong with such designations. They help us map out and measure our experience. Problems emerge when we mistake the designation for the reality it is intended to designate. Then we obsess or over-identify with the "car." In the history of mankind, no obsession has caused more problems than man's tendency to identify with thought. A mind addicted to thought is a self-centered mind and a self-centered mind forces itself upon others. It cannot see the difference between reality and what it thinks about reality.

In a self-centered mind, "I" is the metric upon which the value of everyone and everything is calculated. It is the concept, the *think* that determines the worth of all other things. How someone affects "I" determines whether they are a friend or an enemy. If someone makes us feel warm and bubbly, we see them as good, get attached, and become clingy. On the other hand, if they upset us we call them an asshole. We take the designation so seriously that we fail to see the person.

The self-centered mind fails to realize that what we think of someone is only a measurement of how they make us feel. It does not recognize that they exist independent of what we think. This leads not only to the idea that they are an asshole, but to us treating them like one. We push them away. But no one wants to be pushed away, so they push back. Similarly, no one wants to be smothered. When we cling to them they can't breathe, so they push back to create breathing room. People push back to defend their sovereignty, which self-centeredness ignores. This is conflict. Therefore, the verdict of the ages is that self-centeredness is the root cause of suffering.

The Emptiness of Ego

Every contemplative tradition in the world says that suffering directly results from selfishness and self-centeredness. This is an interesting point: If the sense of self that monopolizes our awareness is more than a designation —that is, if it is a self-existing personality—then spiritual practice amounts to systematic abuse. If the "I" we so readily identify with is a solid, self-existing entity, then spiritual practice—which posits that this self is false and seeks to transcend it—binds us to an unobtainable goal. So let us explore the central hypothesis of contemplative spirituality, the emptiness of ego.

The following exploration is a practice, not a thought experiment. We familiarize ourselves with the line of questioning and bring it to our cushion. The line of questioning is used to search ourselves. In the words of the Hindu saint Ramana Maharshi, "Your duty is to be and not to be this or that. 'I am that I am' sums up the whole truth. The method is summed up in the words 'Be still.' What does stillness mean? It means destroy yourself."[2] The self that is to be destroyed is an illusion and only insight can destroy an illusion. The following inquiry seeks to bring our sight within.

If I removed your arms and legs, hands, fingers, skin, toes, and feet and asked, "Is the 'I' to be found in this part or that part?" you'd respond, "No, 'I' am not the arms, legs, hands, fingers, skin, toes, or feet. 'I' have arms, legs, hands, fingers, skin, toes, and feet. They are parts that belong to 'I.'" So we would press on and investigate the more essential parts, like the eyes, ears, nose, heart, lungs, brain, muscles, and tissues. In each instance I'd ask, "Are you the heart or the eyes, the muscles, nerves or tissues?" And in each instance you'd respond, "I am not the brain or the nervous system, the lungs, or the heart. 'I' have a brain, lungs, nervous system, and heart. 'I' am not the eyes which see, nor the nerves that feel. 'I' possess these things." So, I'd ask, "Are you the act of seeing itself? The hearing? The feeling? The tasting? The smelling? The thinking? Are you the function of these organs?" And you'd respond, "No, 'I' do the seeing, hearing, feeling, tasting, smelling, and thinking. I am watching the movie; I am listening to the radio, or I am thinking, but I am not the act of thinking." But if we look behind the watching, listening, and thinking, we only find more thinking. We see that the sense of self that appears to be watching, listening, and thinking is nothing more than the personification of mental activity.

Finally I would ask, "Are you the decision maker?" This question is a little closer to home. In fact, many would answer,

---

[2] A. L. Herman, *A Brief Introduction to Hinduism: Religion, Philosophy, and Ways of Liberation*, Westview Press (1991), pg. 14

"Yes! I am the decision maker. I decide what to do and when to do it."

When we say "I" is the decision maker, we are saying that "I" is identified with free will. This requires one to believe there is an isolated area of our person—shielded from the influences of both body and environment—where a sovereign entity sits making decisions that effect the course of our life. The illusion of the decision maker starts when the conscious mind is alerted to a course of action determined by the subconscious regions of the brain and body. The conscious mind does participate in the decision making process, but by no means is it a sovereign entity. The conscious mind plays a limited and secondary role in a complex process that involves everything from genetics to environment. The conscious mind does not make decisions. It declares them, which is why it has little power to affect change.

If I were to ask you, "Why do you make decisions that are not in your best interest? Why do you eat unhealthy food or work jobs that stress you out? And more importantly, why do you struggle to change your behavior when you realize that your cholesterol is high or your stress levels are off the charts?" You'd snap back, "Nobody is perfect!" or shrug your shoulders and vapidly respond, "I don't know. I've tried to change those bad habits but I can't." And therein lies the most damning bit of evidence against the existence of a sovereign, autonomous "I." It is powerless. In the famous words of Paul, "I do not do the good I want to do. Instead, I do that which I do not want to do."[3]

There is freedom—complete freedom—but not free will. Freedom is found in the selflessness of the body—in freedom

---

[3] Romans 7:19

from choice. "You see, this thing up here," says Joseph Campbell, "this consciousness, thinks it's running the shop. It's a secondary organ; it's a secondary organ of a total human being, and it must not put itself in control. It must submit and serve the humanity of the body."[4] A healthy ego is an agent, not the principal. It is doing the bidding of the heart. There is no "I" in the control room pulling the levers. At this point in our search we have exhausted all of our parts.

The space once occupied by "I" is revealed to be empty. Much like the car, all that remains is the pile of I-less parts behind us. "I" is a concept held over a network of psychophysical factors that, when aggregated, gives off the appearance of personality. Like a connect-the-dots puzzle, the thinking mind strings together disjointed elements to create the illusion of an autonomous self. But when we search for this personality nothing turns up. This is because the 'thing' we are looking for is actually a 'think.' It is a label, not an answer to the question, "Who am I?"

Though our search came up empty handed, many people continue trying to manufacture a self. They conceive of something otherworldly like the popular notion of a soul, which recasts "I" as an incorporeal entity that inhabits the body, but exists independent of the mind-body complex. Much like the god intelligent design inserts into the equation just before the Big Bang, the existence of such a soul cannot be refuted. But neither can Zeus or Xenu, the dictator of the "Galactic Confederacy" from the Scientology creation story. While the existence of the soul cannot be disproven, its relevance can be called into question.

---

[4] Joseph Campbell, *The Power of Myth*, Doubleday Publishing (2011) Pg. 181

If the soul exists independent from the mind-body complex—neither affected by the psychosomatic structure nor affecting the psychosomatic structure—it has no bearing on our life and is therefore not worthy of our concern. It is disconnected from the reality of our existence. If the soul exists in relationship to the mind-body complex, then it is just another part—no different than any other part in the pile behind us—and therefore not a candidate for the label "I." So once again, we are left with empty space.

The Space is Breathing

If we are willing to sit in this space, instead of filling it with some "think," something interesting happens: we realize the space is alive. It is breathing. It is the process of Being-Itself. Our True Self is the life that flows through the *no-thingness* at the core of our Being, not the names we assign to it. The term True Self can be confusing because the word "self" carries connotations that make it reminiscent of "I." The renowned Jesuit theologian, Pierre Teilhard de Chardin, most eloquently eradicated this confusion when he wrote in *The Divine Milieu*:

> *"And so, for the first time in my life perhaps (although I am supposed to meditate every day!), I took the lamp and, leaving the zone of everyday occupations and relationships where everything seems clear, I went down into my inmost self, to the deep abyss whence I feel dimly that my power of action emanates. But as I moved further and further away from the conventional certainties by which social life is superficially illuminated, I became aware that I was losing contact with myself. At each step of the descent a new person was disclosed within me of whose name I was no*

> *longer sure, and who no longer obeyed me. And when I had to stop my exploration because the path faded from beneath my steps, I found a bottomless abyss at my feet, and out of it came—arising I know not from where—the current which I dare to call my life."*[5]

As strange as it may seem, the True Self is selfless. It is impersonal—free of all the "thinks" that form our habit of personality. The True Self abides in the unconscious depths of the body and does not obey the thinking mind.

When I say the True Self is unconscious, I mean it is unformed—not shaped by thought. The True Self is the unfolding of our human nature into time and space. Since "unfolding" is axiomatically a fluid process, human nature must be formless or flowing. But the True Self is not some disembodied, gnostic blob. Its destiny is inextricably tied to this world.

Who we are cannot be separated from this time and place, the present moment. While our incarnation is not personal, it is individual. Our life's potential has never manifested before, nor will it appear again.[6] "Every man's foremost task," writes Buber, "is the actualization of his unique, unprecedented and never-recurring potentialities, and not the repetition of something that another, and be it even the greatest, has already achieved."[7] The conditions for life gather in this place we call "our body," in this

---

[5] Pierre Teilhard de Chardin, *The Divine Milieu*, Harper Row (1968) pg. 76-77

[6] For this reason we will not be asked, in accounting for our life, so to speak, why we weren't more like Moses, Elijah, Jesus, or the Buddha. We will be asked why we weren't more like our Self.

[7] Martin Buber, *The Way of Man: According to the Teaching of Hasidism,* Citadel Press (1994), pg. 16

instant we call "our life." We are a moment in time. In the limitless Mind of God all possibilities are realized.

"The sacredness, the beauty of each one of us—as a fundamental incarnation of the totality," says Dr. Ray, "is no different from a star or a galaxy or an atom or the whole universe itself." We are a microcosm through which reality incarnates. Our True Life pours forth from the selfless awareness that lives within us as the eternally begotten, unborn Mind of God. This is the "God within me" experience. But this is not the final revelation.

The New Jerusalem

> *Then I saw a new heaven and a new earth, for the old heaven and the old earth had passed away, and the sea was no longer there. Also I saw the holy city, the New Jerusalem, coming down out of heaven from God, prepared like a bride beautifully dressed for her husband. I heard a loud voice from the throne say, "Awaken! God's Presence is with mankind, and he will live with them. They will be his people, and he himself, God-with-them, will be their God." ~ Revelations 21:1-3*

Revelation, or "The Apocalypse," is the final book of the Bible. In popular theology, the word apocalypse is tantamount to a doomsday event. This doomsday is the fetish of every fundamentalist under the sun. To the chagrin of rapturists everywhere, the real meaning of apocalypse is a little more down to earth. The word apocalypse comes to us from the Greek word *apokalyptein*, meaning to "uncover, disclose, or reveal." It exposes something hidden in broad daylight. The book of Revelation *points out* the Kingdom of God, which is literally hidden in *plain sight*.

The author of *Revelation* does not describe the Kingdom as a postmortem utopia populated by immortal spirits. Rather, he says that "the home of God is among mortals." In the final revelation of God, we discover what Meister Eckhart said centuries ago: "The best God ever did for man was to become man himself." In other words, the universe became man. Therefore, the insignia of the New Jerusalem is "Thou art That."[8]

The "God within" experience depends upon the line of demarcation that establishes "within" and "without." This line of demarcation is the division between mind and body. But in basic awareness the external and internal are of "one taste." In the undifferentiated awareness of God, the thinking mind and the body are One Body-One Mind.[9]

When the external world becomes the subject of inquiry, it is revealed to be empty. At the level of direct experience, no amount of effort can verify that the external world exists apart from the field of awareness. This field of awareness is the fabric upon which the whole of creation rests. What we call trees, birds, lovers, friends, enemies, dogs, ships, cars, and horses are manifestations of awareness that arise within the envelope of skin. The whole earth is full of His glory.[10] The philosopher may infer that the external world exists. This inference may be sane, rational, even necessary, but on an experiential level—which is

---

[8] Sanskrit, *Tat Tvam Asi*
[9] John 17:22-23
[10] Isaiah 6:3

the primary concern of spirituality—this extroverted hypothesis can never be verified because all information arises within the limitless sphere of self-existing awareness, including the medium of rational inference, thought.

When we allow thought to be a function of the body—a sensation arising within the expanse of awareness—rather than a superimposed brand of dualistic consciousness, we return the apple, so to speak. We drop the fruit of knowledge and awaken in the Garden, the New Jerusalem.

A Thought in the Mind of God

The New Jerusalem is the union of heaven and earth. The Kingdom is not another world that exists above our delusion. It is the annihilation of our delusion through insight. Just as a flash of lightning disperses darkness, illuminating the dormant landscape, a burst of insight can instantaneously dispel the illusion of duality, revealing the majesty and vitality of the world as-it-is. Revelation is the moment of insight that discloses the underlying unity of the world.

Like "left and right" and "hot and cold," "inner" and "outer" are mutually dependent concepts. The idea of "internal" depends upon "external" and vice versa. They are defined by each other. Since our analysis revealed the external world to be a category of thought, it follows that the internal world is also just a mental designation. When seen from the deep space of basic awareness, there is no inner or outer. The envelope of skin that outlines our person and every sensation that arises within that outline are waves emerging from the ocean of awareness.[11] This

---

[11] "The entire world is ourselves; we ourselves are the entire world. We cannot escape from this fact. Even if there is a place to escape, it can only be enlightenment.

subtle point is illustrated by a story from the Zen tradition:

> *Long ago in China two monks were arguing about a flag blowing in the wind. One monk said, "It is the flag that is moving." The second monk said, "It is the wind that is moving." The Sixth Patriarch came along and said, "You are both wrong. It is not the flag, it is not the wind; it is your mind that is moving."*

The world is the mind and mind is the world; they are not two or even one, but Only. This is the final revelation of God—final, not linearly, but in a circular sense. Remember, spirituality is a process of undoing. It is a return journey. So the final revelation on the path uncovers the first revelation of God—the first day of creation, "Let there be light!"[12] This is the light of God's awareness. And there is One light that shines in all and through all.[13]

The Kingdom is literally hidden in plain sight. It is hidden in basic awareness. When seen through the light of God's awareness, the ordinary is revealed to be the extra-ordinary. The world is set ablaze by the fire of direct experience. The walls are awake, the ground is breathing, and mere mortals shine with the radiance of the sky. It is as if the world is looking back at us through the same eye with which we see it.[14] We live in the Mind of God.

Our body is in the form of the entire world. Indeed, the way of enlightenment and practice of Buddhism can only be grasped by the realization that our skin, flesh, bones, and marrow contain the entire world." — Dogen Zenji, *Shōbōgenzō*,"Komyo"

[12] On the first day of creation, God said, "Let there be light"; and there was light. It wasn't until the fourth day of creation that God made the sun and the moon.

[13] Ephesians 4:6

[14] Meister Eckhart

"There is an instantaneous presence everywhere," writes Plotinus, "nothing containing and nothing left void, everything therefore fully held by the divine."[15] The whole of creation exists within the fullness of God's Will. Awareness is coextensive with reality, meaning that whatever arises—from your beating heart to a thunderstorm—arises out of unborn awareness. There is only awareness.

When we move beyond the artificial sense of self, we hear the "84,000 hymns of praise sung by the mountains and streams."[16] In fact, our life is one of those songs. God doesn't have a will *for* us. There is no checklist or scavenger hunt. God's Will is our very Being. It is Nowness.

In Genesis, it says that humankind was created in the image of God. To say that we were made in the *image* of God is to say that we were formed in the *imagination* of God. We are a thought in the Mind of God.

While we may never permanently abide in this space, we can, through grace and persistence, become more proficient at letting go of self-will and therefore more familiar with living in the Will of God. Undoubtedly this will have a great effect on our quality of life, how we treat others, and the world in which we live. It will transform the world.

Conclusion

The end is here. I have nothing left to say. Words cannot do justice to revelation. Still, I have tried to paint a picture because I like writing. But what we are looking for cannot be

---

[15] *The Ethical Treatises*, "The Divine Mind," Plotinus
[16] Dogen Zenji

found in a book—not in the ramblings of these pages or the masterful works of remarkable minds like Nagarjuna or Thomas Aquinas. Books can be of great assistance, but intellectual knowledge alone will not suffice. Just as faith without works is dead, study without practice is pointless. We must study ourselves.

***

"Pointless! Pointless!" says the Teacher.
"Utterly pointless! Everything is meaningless."
A generation goes, and a generation comes,
but the world remains forever.
The sun rises and the sun goes down,
and hurries to the place where it rises.
The wind blows to the south,
and goes around to the north;
round and round goes the wind,
and on its circuits the wind returns.
All streams run to the sea,
but the sea is not full;
to the place where the streams flow,
there they continue to flow.
All words are wearisome;
more than one can express;
the eye is not satisfied with seeing,
or the ear filled with hearing.
What has been is what will be,
and what has been done is what will be done;
there is nothing new under the sun.[17]

---

[17] Ecclesiastes 1:4-9

ABOUT THE AUTHOR

Benjamin Riggs is a meditation teacher, author, and columnist. He lives in Shreveport, Louisiana where he serves as the director of the Refuge Meditation Group.

Connect with Ben at:
FindingGodInTheBody.com
Facebook.com/FindingGodInTheBody
Twitter.com/Benjamin_Riggs

For more information about workshops, retreats, and speaking engagements please visit:
findinggodinthebody.com/about-the-author